ADVERTISING WORKS

ADVERTISING WORKS

Papers from the IPA Advertising Effectiveness Awards

Institute of Practitioners in Advertising, 1980

Edited and introduced by

Simon Broadbent

1981

HOLT, RINEHART AND WINSTON

LONDON · NEW YORK · SYDNEY · TORONTO

Publishers to the Advertising Association

Holt, Rinehart and Winston Ltd: 1 St Anne's Road
Eastbourne, East Sussex BN21 3UN

British Library Cataloguing in Publication Data

Broadbent, Simon
  Advertising works.
  1. Advertising—Great Britain—Case studies
  I. Title
  659.1'11   HF5808.G7

ISBN 0-03-910322-6

Typeset, printed and bound in Great Britain by Butler & Tanner Ltd, Frome and London

Last digit is print number: 9 8 7 6 5 4 3 2 1

Contents

SECTION 3 DIRECT RESPONSE, CONSUMER GOODS AND SERVICES 153

SECTION 4 INDUSTRIAL AND FINANCIAL   181

IPA
Advertising Effectiveness Awards

In the spring of 1980, management and trade publications carried an unusual advertisement. It offered prizes worth £16 000 in a competition:

ADVERTISING WORKS
AND WE'RE GOING TO PROVE IT

In the advertising business we all know that the ultimate test of any advertising campaign is the sales result to which it contributes. Sadly this hard truth is not always well acknowledged outside the agency world where the accountability of advertising is held in some doubt.

The Institute of Practitioners in Advertising is now setting out to remedy this situation with a unique competitive award scheme that will be based solely on the assessment of the *effects* of advertising campaigns in any media. It will aim to achieve three things:

1 A better understanding of the crucial role advertising plays in marketing.

2 Closer analysis of advertising effectiveness and improved methods of evaluation.

3 A clear demonstration that advertising can be proven to work, against measurable criteria.

At the same time, leaflets were sent out to IPA agencies. They too announced the competition, gave the entry rules, and added a guide to authors:

The difficulties of separating the effect of advertising from other parts of the marketing mix are well known: nonetheless the key requirement in this award scheme is to build an individual case whose results, methodology and presentation are the most convincing, in the judges' opinion, in establishing the positive effects of a particular strategy and execution.

Demonstrating the cost-effectiveness of any given campaign would obviously help to make a case even more strongly, but it is understood that a demonstration of payout may be impractical, for a number of reasons. Likewise, it is accepted that certain figures may have to be given as indices, to preserve confidentiality. However, it is hoped that the measurement criteria will be as 'hard' as possible, involving behavioural evidence such as sales, rather than attitude or awareness shifts, unless such indications really are the most relevant.

The methods of campaign evaluation should be fully described as it is the demonstration of how the advertising was shown to work which is required, as much as a description of the strategy and its results.

Winning papers will probably meet both of these criteria: they will describe marketing successes in which advertising played a full part; they will also be clearly and persuasively presented.

The exact format of the papers is not specified, but it is expected that many entries will cover:

—Business background

—Marketing and advertising objectives

—Description of the campaign, including creative and media strategies; it is not essential to show the executions in the paper, but they should be described (this may be supplemented by audio-visual material but the description should be sufficient without it)

—Campaign evaluation

—Conclusions on the success or otherwise of the campaign, on the way the advertising worked and on the methods used.

The awards scheme was enthusiastically supported at all levels in the IPA, which is concerned about the way advertising is seen by industry, Government and the media.

It is the IPA's belief that advertising can be a major element in the marketing mix. It is a serious commercial tool. It can be a contributor to profit, handsomely repaying investment in it. It is not a cost, irrelevant to sales volume and drawing direct on the profit at the bottom of the balance sheet, as accountants sometimes treat it.

Waiting for the response from agencies was an anxious time. Would enough advertisers agree to release details of strategy and perhaps sales? Did agencies in fact believe sufficiently seriously in these high standards of campaign evaluation? Were they confident enough that their work produced measurable results? Would authors give the required time to write satisfactory papers? Although there was no precedent to work to, would the papers prove convincing?

On 30th June, the closing date, these questions were all answered 'yes'. The total number of entries was 80, from over 30 agencies.

The panel of judges had previously been prepared with the criteria they were to apply and knew how they had to work. In two months, they had to sift out the winners, recommend an overall winner and decide which others were worth commendation. Long letters evaluating the entries were exchanged, papers rose and fell in the lists.

Stephen King, one of the judges, recorded his approach to the assessment of the new product category. The note he circulated is worth quoting in full, which I do with his permission:

1. The award is for demonstration

Whatever the problem of getting foolproof briefs for awards, the spirit of this exercise is quite clear. What is required is a *convincing demonstration* that advertising has worked, expressed in some way relevant to business objectives. So ...

(a) I will give highest marks to papers that *demonstrate* the contribution best – not necessarily the campaigns I think have contributed most. The *evaluation method* is critical.

(b) The effectiveness should be in terms of *business results* (e.g. profits, sales, share of market), not intermediate measures (e.g. awareness, attitude change, recall).

(c) My overall ranking will reflect the order in which I feel papers would get the response from *people outside advertising*: 'That really makes me believe that advertising has an economic effect.'

2. Advertising's contribution to launching new brands

One problem with this category of entry is that, by definition, new brands start off with no sales, no usage, no awareness, no attitudes. Thus a presentation that simply shows increases in all these does not seem to me to *demonstrate* advertising effectiveness, except in a totally trivial way. Of course all the measures go up (there's no other direction) and of course most manufacturers would not contemplate a launch without advertising.

In my view, to qualify for an award the entry has to demonstrate that launch advertising has caused sales, usage, etc., to go up *more than might have been expected*. That is, there has to be some form of *comparison* – with previous experience of new brands, the 'norms' of existing brands, different regions, different time periods, the same money spent in another way, 'econometrics', etc.

In other words, I think there needs to be a demonstration of a *particularly successful* launch; not an assertion that one cannot launch a new brand without advertising.

3. Advertising's contribution to the successful establishment of a new brand

The post-launch situation seems rather different. The evidence is that the key to success in a new brand is its repeat-purchase rate, and that this depends on the response of triers to it as a totality. The brand has to be 'better and different'. If triers like its *blend of physical and psychological values*, they'll go on buying it and paying a reasonable price for it.

Our rules mention the difficulty of disentangling the effect of advertising from that of other marketing activities. For new brands, it seems to me not simply difficult to do, but actually wrong to try. In a sense, for a new brand, the advertising *is* the brand.

Maybe its most important objective is to contribute a *distinct personality* to the new brand as the basis for the brand's saleability – that is, its long term ability to sustain sales at a price premium or a profitable price.

To some extent therefore, if the brand becomes established as a successful business proposition, the advertising *must* have succeeded. But it is very hard to see how this can be *demonstrated*. Maybe blind versus named product tests, in demonstrating brand values, could be said to measure advertising contribution. Maybe demonstrations of price premium are evidence.

I think we may have to use a fair amount of judgement in assessing this (qualitative) contribution from advertising. Papers will of course have to demonstrate that the brand as a whole (i.e. the blend of advertising, product, packaging, etc.) is distinctive, profitable, successful, etc.

4. Analysis of entries

In line with these thoughts I will try to analyse entries under these headings.

(a) *Advertising's contribution to business objectives*

Demonstration method. What measurements were used and how sensible/convincing they are; how 'hard' the measurements are.

Comparison. What experiment or comparisons were used.

(b) *Advertising's contribution to the brand's saleability*

Brand personality. How distinct, how much advertising contributes.

Demonstration method. How the brand's saleability is measured.

(c) *Quality of the entry*

Line of argument. What it is; how convincing it is.

Presentation. How clear, interesting, readable, convincing, etc.

The IPA felt that the most useful examinations of how consumers are affected by advertising follow an explicit strategy statement. The purpose of the advertising must be clear both to the creative department and to the researcher designing an evaluation. The evidence from this collection is that marketing and advertising strategies are very often well thought through and clearly expressed. Considered only as a set of examples of campaign planning and advertising development, this book is well worth study.

The judges looked carefully at this aspect and had a checklist which read:

Is the market and business background within which the campaign is designed to operate adequately but succinctly described?

Are the advertiser's marketing objectives clearly stated, with the role of advertising in achieving them, and how this integrates with other marketing activity?

Are specific objectives stated for the advertising?

Is the target audience defined?

Are the research measures made relevant to the objective?

Are the measurements adequately described? Were they properly carried out?

The judges also looked for logic in the arguments and clarity of expression. Unless it is reasonably presented, the best case fails to convince.

The judges' work was completed at a long meeting on 2nd September. They had examined 24 entries for New Consumer Products and 37 for Established Consumer Products. Clearly these are the fields where most evaluation work is done – at least, that which may be published.

Direct response drew only six entries; though these campaigns were presumably the most measurable, the evidence here also contains most direct help to competitors. Many agencies must be sitting on very hard data about the sales turnover for which advertising is responsible.

Industrial gave us five entries and Financial eight. These categories did not produce the same level of entry as the consumer products. This is not just because of a lower advertising spend justifying less research, for some of the low budget consumer cases demonstrated considerable and careful data analysis. Advertising is arguably more peripheral to these sorts of companies than to the mainstream consumer goods manufacturers. The latter often spend five or ten per cent of their turnover on advertising. More importantly, brand differentiation and positioning often depend critically on advertising. The agency can be an equal partner in strategy determination, in planning and in research. This involvement and a sense of concern for the product showed in the best consumer entries but was generally lacking in the other categories. Perhaps a study of the work for their consumer goods neighbours will encourage industrialists and financiers to draw their agencies closer.

Consumer products also benefit in a competition like this because sales data for a brand – whether ex-factory or as recorded in an audit – are reasonably 'hard'. So are consumer research results on a single brand. For industrial and financial products, this clarity is often lacking. Further, because sales data and marketing policies are less obvious or public, confidentiality is more of a problem.

These are only difficulties in showing advertising to be effective. It is hoped that in future competitions some way will be found to prove the value of advertising in industrial, financial, recruitment and other fields.

The awards were announced on 23rd September. No prizes were given in the last two categories for the reasons outlined. This does not, of course, imply that advertising is not as effective in these categories, only that its demonstration was not as convincing.

There were eight prizewinners and 18 commended papers. All these papers and their authors are listed below. From these 26 I have chosen 18 for this book. The main criteria for selection were to show the variety of tasks which advertising can tackle and the range of methods used to evaluate it. I have had to exclude, for reasons of space, some excellent entries. The papers here are not printed exactly as submitted, but have been edited for clarification and to reduce some of the supporting material not immediately relevant to campaign evaluation.

The most significant difference from the entries is that only one or two examples of the advertising are given here for each paper. The submissions included many scripts, tapes, press advertisements, display material and so on. These played no part in the judges' assessments. To win an effectiveness award may or may not involve creative work which receives the approval of the creative world – though the chances are that it will. Equally, to win a creative award may or may not mean a good sales result – though again it probably does. The two sorts of criteria are neither identical nor incompatible: they serve different purposes.

IPA ADVERTISING EFFECTIVENESS AWARDS WORKING PARTY

Chris Hawes, Chairman, Davidson Pearce
(*Chairman of the IPA Marketing Group*)

Simon Broadbent, Vice-Chairman, Leo Burnett
(*Chairman of the Working Party*)

Mike Stepan, Director, Benton & Bowles

Alan Wolfe, Marketing Services Director, Ogilvy & Mather

JUDGES

Professor John Treasure, The City University, Business School
(*Chairman*)

Simon Broadbent, Leo Burnett

Peter Gittoes, Barclays Bank Ltd

Anthony Gould Davies, Gould Davies Ltd

Stephen King, J. Walter Thompson

Gilbert Lamb, Tube Investments Ltd

Professor Ken Simmonds, London Business School

ACKNOWLEDGEMENTS

The success of the Awards is in no small measure due to the publications which gave free advertising space for promoting the scheme, and whose help is gratefully acknowledged:

Admap   *Media World*
Campaign   *Now!*
Daily Telegraph *Observer*
Evening News   *Sunday Times*
Financial Times *Talking Points*
Marketing   *The Times*
Marketing Week

Many people at the Institute of Practitioners in Advertising worked on this scheme, but it owes most to the untiring efforts of Janet Mayhew, Research Officer, Secretary to the Marketing Group and the Working Party, of Julia Steell, assistant to the Research Officer, and of John Foster, Public Relations Officer.

Prizes and Commendations

NEW PRODUCTS, CONSUMER GOODS AND SERVICES

FIRST PRIZE AND GRAND PRIX

How advertising helped make Krona brand leader
Stephen Benson
> *Davidson Pearce* for *Van der Berghs*

SECOND PRIZES

The case for All Clear shampoo
Gil McWilliam
> *J. Walter Thompson* for *Elida Gibbs*

Whitegates: a regional success story
David A. Blythe
> *Bowden, Dyble & Hayes* for *Whitegates Estate Agency*

CERTIFICATES OF COMMENDATION

The effect of television advertising on the launch of Deep Clean
Andrew Roberts, Mark Hilder and Julian English
> *D'Arcy-MacManus & Masius* for *Reckitt Household and Toiletry Products*

Yorkie: a new chocolate bar
John Williams
> *J. Walter Thompson* for *Rowntree Mackintosh*

Cornetto: introducing a big brand
Rod Meadows
> *Lintas* for *Walls Ice Cream*

The role of the advertising for Listerine and Listermint
Terry Bullen
  J. Walter Thompson for *Warner Lambert*

Lilt: a case history
Ian Woolgar
  Wasey Campbell-Ewald for *The Coca-Cola Export Corporation*

ESTABLISHED PRODUCTS: CONSUMER GOODS AND SERVICES

FIRST PRIZE

Dettol: a case history
Angus Thomas, Andrew Roberts, Gerard Smith & Mia Ospovat
  D'Arcy-MacManus & Masius for *Reckitt & Colman Pharmaceutical Division*

SECOND PRIZE

Kellogg's Rice Krispies: the effect of a new creative execution
Jeremy Elliott
  J. Walter Thompson for *Kellogg Co. of Great Britain*

CERTIFICATES OF COMMENDATION

The repositioning of Lucozade
Mike Soden and Michael Stewart
  Leo Burnett for *Beecham Foods*

Shloer: increase in sales as a result of a media change
Elizabeth Leffman and Michael Stewart
  J. Walter Thompson for *Beecham Foods*

Swan Vesta matches
Nigel Beard
  Doyle Dane Bernbach for *Bryant & May*

An evaluation of the effectiveness of the current Campari campaign
Frances Foster
  J. Walter Thompson for *Findlater Matta*

Mini in 1979
Sandy Johnston and Lynne Sacks
  Leo Burnett for *BL Europe and Overseas*

The effect of advertising on Sanatogen Multivitamins
Michael Brugman
  McCormick Intermarco-Farner for *Fisons*

Pretty Polly
B. I. D. McMeekin
  Collett Dickenson Pearce for *Pretty Polly*

Cheese: effective use of advertising to increase consumption
Peter Bear
  Harrison McCann Advertising for *Cheese Information Service*

DIRECT RESPONSE: CONSUMER GOODS AND SERVICES

FIRST PRIZE

The launch of Tjaereborg Rejser
Damian O'Malley
  The Boase Massimi Pollitt Univas Partnership for *Tjaereborg Rejser*

SECOND PRIZES

The British Film Institute and advertising effectiveness
Richard Block
  Ogilvy & Mather for *The British Film Institute*

Royal Air Force officer recruitment
James Goble
  J. Walter Thompson for *Central Office of Information*

CERTIFICATE OF COMMENDATION

The Triumph Dolomite Autumn 1978 Test Drive campaign
Gary Duckers
  Saatchi & Saatchi Garland Compton for *BL Cars*

INDUSTRIAL

CERTIFICATE OF COMMENDATION

Lucas Aerospace 'Eagle' campaign
Keith Nicklin and Michael Smithwick
  Nicklin Advertising for *Lucas Aerospace*

FINANCIAL AND OTHER NON-CONSUMER GOODS AND SERVICES

CERTIFICATES OF COMMENDATION

Halifax Building Society Convertible Term Shares
F. T. Howe
  Brunning Advertising & Marketing (Yorkshire) for *Halifax Building Society*

The launch of Abbey National Open Bondshares
Tom Vaughan
  Lonsdale Advertising for *Abbey National Building Society*

Comments on Campaign Evaluation

Helping to design this competition, reading the entries and above all learning from the views of the other judges was a fruitful experience. It provoked some thoughts on campaign evaluation which are recorded here. An analysis of the methods used in these papers has been added, to help those who would like a checklist of current practice.

WHAT IS EVALUATED

Of course sales are affected by many factors other than advertising. This collection gives examples: the quality of the product, its price, distribution and promotions, total consumers' spending, seasonality, competitive activity and so on.

In a proper evaluation of advertising these factors must be measured and taken into account. They can be allowed for, either in a well-designed test or by statistical methods or in a commonsense way. When they are examined carefully we may learn a great deal to our advantage. For example, we may see the sales effects of those other factors we can influence, like price, and hence we see how to raise our efficiency. We will also be able to make improved sales forecasts. It is hard to give a convincing demonstration of advertising's sales effectiveness without discussing these other factors, though many of the entrants tried.

In the campaigns themselves there are examples here of the four main actions which can be evaluated:

—a single campaign idea (as in a launch or when a brand has had consistent advertising for some time),
—a change in the advertising strategy,
—a change in the amount spent on advertising,
—changes in the media used.

There is a difference between evaluating new and established brands. For a new product, advertising is probably at its most effective (when it works well). In creating awareness, saying something new, positioning the brand and encouraging trial it has obvious tasks and opportunities. The job to be done is easier in some ways than when a brand is well known. When an advertised new brand succeeds, it is, however, hard to identify the reasons for its success. The whole mix has to be right and isolating advertising's effect is a delicate task. So while the work is more rewarding, its evaluation is more difficult.

1

For an established brand, there is a history with which our latest results can be compared; the effects of other factors can usually be allowed for. With new products no comparisons are possible, except with other, different new products; there are too little data on which to study the effects of the various factors.

It was perhaps natural that it was the established brands in this competition which produced the largest number of convincing evaluations.

THE ATTITUDE TO EVALUATION

A characteristic found in the best plans and evaluation reports is a nice mixture of optimism and caution. Optimism in that the advertising was undertaken with enthusiasm and single-minded determination. Caution anticipates that other causes will affect the results; it plans experiments or analyses which test these possibilities. It also tempers the optimism with the admission that the advertising may sometimes be less effective than we hoped.

A researcher or planner helps his team most when he approaches evaluation like a barrister anticipating possible difficult questions in cross-examination or like a scientist trying to disprove the hypothesis he wishes to support. The hypothesis is of course that advertising creates and supports sales, the objection is that all sales can be explained in other ways. The whole team should welcome being held accountable, they should be ready to put their beliefs to the test.

The team should also be open-minded and eager to learn. From the papers published here the reader might gather that confirmation of our point of view is always obtained. He must remember that these are success stories, and is warned that in practice the results are not always what he expects. An evaluation which shows a campaign to be a failure and from which a new worthwhile campaign arises is just as useful though unlikely to be entered in this competition.

Management's attitude to evaluation has generally been sceptical. Management often believes that advertising cannot produce measurable results, but these papers show that it can. Management is more properly doubtful about whether evaluation is worth doing, whether the cost of data collection and time in analysis are likely enough to pay off. From the examples given here, it can be seen how often evaluation is worthwhile and how subsequent decisions can be improved.

Management is also concerned about generalization and the validity of projection. It is not enough to find out the reasons for past success or failure; we need to improve future decisions. Unfortunately, what we learn about this brand this year may not help another brand or even this brand next year. However, the marketing environment does not usually change so fast that we cannot apply what we have learned. Also, the more we understand the real world the better will our judgement become.

TWO TYPES OF EVALUATION

Campaign evaluation helps to answer two groups of questions. The first set are about what it did and the second about how it worked:

First:

      Can the sales effect of the advertising be estimated?

      Was advertising profitable?

Second:

How were consumers affected?

How were other parts of the mix affected by advertising – trade, distribution, etc.?

and finally:

Are all the different results consistent?

Do they confirm our strategy?

In the most useful evaluations both sorts of question are raised: we approach the job from several angles. It was a welcome discovery that in many cases here a range of methods was indeed used. It is always prudent to try every affordable way, to bracket the truth and to get as deep an appreciation of the market as possible.

The advertiser who receives a wide-ranging evaluation gets guidance on the size of his future advertising budget (and on the decisions he has to make about other marketing funds). He learns why and how the results were reached; he increases his knowledge of the tools at his disposal. Specifically, he is guided on how to improve creative work, scheduling, area and media choice and so on.

Profitability of the advertising investment as measured in these examples is more impressive when it is realized that the sums here are about a short term return on advertising: the changes produced over months and so, usually, in the current financial year. Possible benefits in the creation or maintenance of a brand are not here credited to advertising.

The longer term contribution of advertising may be greater than in the current year – and this is particularly likely for a new brand, for which a one- or even two-year payoff cannot often be expected. It is hard to imagine some of the famous brands examined below reaching their present positions without the help of past advertising in positioning them, explaining their use, giving them a personality. This competition confirmed that few if any people have techniques which they trust to evaluate advertising's results over several years.

There is no one method to evaluate a campaign, for this collection emphasizes that there can be many different advertising objectives and ways in which the advertising is expected to work. The most common combination of methods is a single, sales-based measure (change on last year, area test or statistical analysis) with consumer usage and attitude data which help us to see how the advertising affected people and why a sales change or its maintenance are credible.

It was less welcome to find from the entries overall that the most common single method used by agencies is simple association: we did this, sales or consumer measures did that.

It is obvious that half the brand shares in any one year will increase (ignoring own label, launches and so on), and in those markets where there is volume growth, a high proportion of marketing activity is always associated with sales success in some form. This is hardly proof of cause and effect.

Support from other data sources, or a more thorough analysis, or the elimination of other factors, or all of these, are required for a totally convincing demonstration of this kind. Association over a short period is not really enough. This comment applies in two ways. An agency which claims, without other evidence, that its advertising contributed to a sales increase which happened at the same time is on shaky ground (which will be revealed if the increase was actually due to other causes). An advertiser who blames his agency during a sales decline, without other evidence, is equally weak statistically but unfortunately rather more powerful commercially.

Equally, consumer attitudes may change along the lines intended by the advertising strategy without any effect on sales necessarily following. When you lead the horse to water and it does not drink, have you failed? The agency can claim that if it agreed a task with the advertiser – to be noticed or to change a particular attitude – and achieved it, then though sales may have been disappointing the advertising cannot be blamed.

The conclusion is logical, but the premise can be challenged, assuming that the reason for sales failure was a factor known when the strategy was agreed. Could the strategy have been right, if achieving its objectives did not lead to satisfactory sales? Should not the agency take responsibility for strategy?

These are difficult questions. It is for such reasons that many practitioners sincerely believe that campaigns cannot be properly evaluated.

This collection shows that, when the strategy is correct, this trap can be avoided. Advertising's association with sales (which might otherwise be treated as random) can be tested. The effects of advertising can be better understood.

ANALYSIS OF METHODS USED

The methods used to evaluate the campaigns are now classified, and some other techniques not used in this collection are also mentioned.

No standardization of methods is to be expected. The analogy is not with quality control, every campaign meeting the same criteria, but with a workbench from which the most relevant tools are chosen to meet whatever practical objectives have been set when the strategy was drawn up.

The major division in methods is whether sales volume itself is analysed (i.e. where profit was generated) or whether consumer reactions are studied (i.e. how these sales came about). The emphasis in this competition was on advertising paying its way, so there are more examples here of the first type; in general the second type is much more frequent.

Within sales methods, four main types are identified (Sections 1 to 4 below), within consumer reactions, two (Sections 5.1 and 5.2). The classifications are not exclusive: a blend of methods is normal. Naming a case history as exemplifying one method is only drawing attention to this aspect: other methods often appear in each example.

SALES MEASURES

1. Area Tests

1.1.   AREA TESTS WHICH ALLOW STATISTICALLY FOR THE EFFECTS OF OTHER FACTORS

The two examples here are both of Beecham's AMTES. The analysis of an area test is preceded by a study of the other measurable factors which brand management believes affect sales. In these two cases the factors are distribution, competitors' distribution, price, competitors' price, temperature and new claims to sickness benefit. The way these factors have contributed to area differences in the past, plus their values during the test, are then used to estimate how much of any subsequent difference between areas is due to them and therefore how much remains to be attributed to the variable tested. The result of an area test can be accepted with much more confidence when we know the other factors have been taken into account. The tests were a copy change in the case of Lucozade and additional TV advertising for Shloer.

Area tests usually measure the direct consumer effect of advertising only. Other ways advertising affects marketing are not reproduced exactly in a small area. For example, a test of zero advertising weight in an area may result in a smaller sales decline than if we withdrew all advertising nationally, since such action over the whole country might produce trade and competitor reactions we do not provoke by a local change.

This comment points out a relatively small, and only potential, defect in area testing. Its great virtue is that it is a deliberate experiment and therefore its findings are free of much of the statistical uncertainty which clouds the analysis of naturally occurring results.

1.2. AREA TESTS WHICH DO NOT ALLOW EXPLICITLY FOR OTHER FACTORS

Area tests are usually carried out without other factors being formally taken into account. Presumably a commonsense check is made that they did not alter so much as to put the test in doubt.

For a new brand the use of a test area may not be to check alternative copy or weight, but (as with Krona) simply as a miniature of the whole of the UK: a test market in the classical sense.

For a new brand (Tjaereborg) or an existing one (Sanatogen), the TV areas may be receiving support in addition to other national activity. We may then be able to calculate the additional sales produced by the additional advertising. Often sales are more responsive to advertising during launch or when new activity is undertaken so it is wise to insist on a clearly profitable result before proceeding later nationally.

1.3. AREA TESTS INCLUDING CALCULATION OF THE EFFECT OVER TIME

The effect of advertising can sometimes be estimated over the months following that in which it appeared. The normal method is to assume that its effect decays exponentially. In one paper (Deep Clean) the amount by which sales in the test areas differed from national sales was studied over time. It was found that sales did indeed revert over time towards the national pattern and it was possible to estimate how long the sales effect lasted. This is hardly a normal analysis but an extremely useful one which confirms other evidence on how the effects of advertising diminish over time. When this delay is ignored and the results of a test are cut off too early we underestimate advertising's results.

2. Statistical Analysis

2.1. MULTIPLE REGRESSION, ALLOWING FOR THE EFFECT OF SEVERAL FACTORS

The only example in this collection of a classical econometric analysis is in the Dettol paper. The other factors considered (besides advertising weight) were disposable income, price and seasonal variation. Together, these four accounted for 90 per cent of sales volume variation.

Such work is not to be lightly undertaken, for there are pitfalls in the statistical analysis of time series with a number of variables which may themselves be correlated. The methods are complex, which does not make them suspect. Many will find it hard to follow the argument but their efforts will be rewarded.

One among several results in this case was an estimate of how much sales changed when advertising weight was changed; the qualitative aspect of the advertising is shown in the amount of change. From the costs and other budget details it is shown that advertising returned in profit more than was invested in it. Cutting the advertising budget would have meant less profit, increasing it would have meant more.

The claim to have measured this profitable result is a very strong one. It is supported and explained in this case by the other measurements made.

2.2. EXAMINING THE EFFECT OF OTHER VARIABLES SEPARATELY

The All Clear example does not carry out a simultaneous analysis of the effects of the factors thought to explain sales variations, but it does examine them singly. Price, a consumer promotion, a trade promotion, distribution and competitive activity were all looked at. The analysis is by inspection rather than by regression, and concludes that sales variations were not dependent on them. Advertising weight and seasonality are put forward as the reasons for sales variation. The size of the advertising effect is numerically estimated and by implication (though profit is not revealed) the advertising return is evaluated.

2.3. ESTIMATE OF THE EFFECT OF PRICE AND ADVERTISING

The third example which explicitly takes a factor besides advertising into account numerically is Rice Krispies. The other variable considered is price, usually a much more important factor than advertising. It is studied by a classical economist's demand analysis, plotting sales share against relative price. Two separate time periods are considered, the second after the new advertising started, at a comparable advertising weight to the earlier period. The average relationship between sales and price shifted convincingly to the right, as economic text books lead us to expect when the perceived value of the product is raised.

The overall variety of marketing situations is well illustrated by the comparison of the high price elasticity here (-2) with the Dettol low (-0.2).

2.4. ANALYSIS OF AREA VARIATIONS

TV areas can be considered as a set of test markets. In each area a different advertising weight may be applied and the results observed.

This may be the result of deliberate policy, following an experimental pattern which allows a thorough examination of the sales effect of advertising, perhaps over a number of brands. At least one advertiser sets his advertising budgets this way, continually testing at different levels.

The Swan Vestas paper is not so ambitious, but shows convincingly that greater sales increases occurred where advertising weight was higher.

2.5. DYNAMIC DIFFERENCE

This technique has been known for many years, as the Rice Krispies paper which uses it points out, but it deserves wider use than it gets. At the least, it is a useful way of recording the history of a brand (or more usually of a number of brands in a market). The plot described in the paper shows how brand share changes are related to advertising share.

Notice how, as in the other Rice Krispies analysis, relative numbers are compared, not absolutes, as with Dettol.

Weaknesses of dynamic difference are that other factors are not explicitly examined and that some of the relationship may not be advertising causing sales but vice versa. Perhaps, when we knew we were gaining share for some other reason such as improved distribution, a rule such as a constant advertising to sales ratio led to increased advertising at the same time. These possible defects can of course be allowed for by the people using the system.

Once a regularity has been observed it can be used in various ways:

—to indicate the budget required for a particular sales change,
—by comparing brands, to see whether ours has an inherent advantage or disadvantage (its line is above or below other brands),
—to detect anomalies: as here, a higher brand share change than expected for the advertising investment, hence an indication that advertising had improved efficiency or some other improvement had taken place.

2.6. CALCULATION OF A LAGGED ADVERTISING EFFECT

In the Dettol and Deep Clean examples the effect of advertising is assumed to be spread over all subsequent periods, decaying exponentially. A simpler but similar assumption is that it works in the current and subsequent period only. This is the method in the RAF recruitment paper, where display advertising 'last' month contributes some enquiries 'this' month but fewer than does advertising in 'this' month.

In this particular example two sorts of advertising are also distinguished: display and classified.

The regression coefficients when these advertising factors are compared with enquiries indicate how much advertising's effect is lagged and also how much display and classified each contribute.

3. Non-statistical Analysis

3.1. EXAMINING THE EFFECT OF OTHER VARIABLES SEPARATELY

The Mini paper is an example of judging a campaign by a sales criterion and listing other factors which might have influenced the result, without a numerical analysis. This must be done when suitable data on other factors are hard to come by.

3.2. PRE-POST SALES DIFFERENCE

In the Halifax example a sales difference is claimed without other factors in the market being explicitly listed and evaluated. Perhaps these were known to the advertiser and agency and just happen not to be published in the paper.

3.3. ASSOCIATION OF SALES AND ADVERTISING PATTERNS

When the advertising has had clear peaks over time and is expected to bring in sales soon after appearance, it is reasonable to look for an association with the pattern of sales over time. This is the way the RAF recruitment example is presented graphically. Although a multiple regression was carried out, the reader is invited to compare the rate of enquiries with a lagged advertising pattern to convince himself that advertising had an effect. Unless such a connection can be seen in the data, it is hard to demonstrate it to the advertiser.

Campari and Whitegates come into this category, though with more convincing support from other directions as to why the changes occurred.

4.   Direct Response

4.1.   COUPONS, BROCHURE REQUESTS, CONVERSIONS

The classical direct response measure is when coupons are cut from press advertising – and conversions are also recorded. In particular, as in the Halifax example, media efficiency can be measured very precisely. The BFI paper shows creative effectiveness being measured too. Especially when there are no other marketing tools or sales outlets, this method can show advertising's results incontrovertibly.

For Tjaereborg the efficiency of such a media operation is interestingly compared with conventional outlets to its advantage.

4.2.   RESPONSE CARDS

In the technical press a magazine is rather like a shop window. Sending for more details through a reader response service is like walking into the shop. The Lucas example shows these data being used to help creative decisions and to check the geographical spread of the campaign. In such a case media are, of course, only a part of a selling operation and the smaller its share (contrasted with its overwhelming importance to the Tjaereborg launch) the harder it is to evaluate.

5.   Consumer Measures

When we turn to interviews with people in our target we should separate their responses about the product from their responses about the advertising.

5.1.   PRODUCT RESEARCH

The most frequent check on consumers is the regular usage and attitude survey. Whether they claim to buy the brand, what they use it for, what they think of it – methods to measure these are reasonably well established.

Certainly the Campari case shows that the sales increase noted could hardly have occurred separately from the new usage which the advertising was designed to encourage. The Dettol example also shows changes in perception following strategy. The Lucozade relaunch was followed by an increase in the reason for purchase which the advertising was intended to stimulate. In the Shloer area tests awareness increased as well as sales and the new purchasers could be identified by age, which overall sales turnover can of course never tell us.

The Krona evaluation gives several examples of reassuring information gathered from housewives during the launch. It would have been helpful in this case to have been given norms against which the details of the launch were compared and which could have been used early in the launch to estimate eventual brand share, but this is a counsel of perfection.

What all these examples have in common is the guidance they offered the agency on which parts of their execution seemed to be working and which parts might be improved. This function can never be fulfilled by sales data. They also help the marketer to see why changes in sales are taking place, which otherwise might be dismissed as due to other factors.

In these papers the part played by regular tracking studies (as opposed to irregular surveys) is under-represented. These can give a greater chance to measure dynamics, to see what happens after we stop advertising, to isolate periods of special importance (e.g. when a competitor retaliates) and so on. Group discussions also feature little, but have a useful purpose in monitoring consumer change as well as being an opportunity to try out the next idea.

5.2. ADVERTISING RESEARCH

In addition to asking consumers about products, we can ask them about advertising. This runs the risk of being self-indulgent and irrelevant so is given here after sales and opinions about the product. It has its merits though.

Advertising awareness is not an end in itself but being consciously noticed is often a necessary requirement and a useful check (if it is low there is often something wrong). Details of the advertising recalled are very helpful both to strategy and to execution. The Lucas example shows the reassurance this can give. Tjaereborg measured as well as product information the medium where the brand was first heard of. The reader should be warned that television often scores here more prominently than its actual use.

Day-after recall is more used in the United States than here. When it is merely one of a battery of tests during campaign development, and its limitations are appreciated (as in the Lucozade example), it has its place. It should never feature on its own in campaign evaluation.

6. Other Effects

[handwritten annotation: does this mean the day after recall or advertising research?]

In addition to its effects on the consumer, advertising can be seen to have results elsewhere. Being admired in the business (creative acclaim) or liked by the advertisers' sales force or Board is not evidence of sales effectiveness. Recognition in the retail trade is a stronger clue, and successful use of the creative material in promotions and competitions (see the Pretty Polly example) shows it working in additional ways, which may well be valuable when such activities help in gaining distribution and trade acceptance. These are additional uses of the advertising which escape measurement in the conventional manner but may be real and appreciated for all that.

CONCLUSION

This brief guide to the papers does not describe all that the reader can learn from them. The most valuable opportunity in case histories is that we can share in the experience of the team behind the campaign. I would like to thank the advertisers and the authors for this privilege.

Section One

New Products, Consumer Goods and Services

1

How Advertising Helped Make Krona Brand Leader

INTRODUCTION

This case history analyses the launch of Krona margarine, a new product from Van den Berghs, into the Harlech and Westward TV areas.

The brand was sold in from 9th October 1978 and TV advertising broke on 20th October 1978. The case history covers a period of twelve months from launch in the two test areas.

Krona was launched to exploit the widening gap in price between butter and margarine and to attract butter users who were trading down. The brand succeeded beyond all expectations and by the end of the first year was established as brand leader in the launch areas with a national equivalent turnover of £32m at RSP.

Following this successful test market Krona has been extended to other areas. In all but one of these Krona is now brand leader or Number 2 brand.

Substantial problems existed in promoting Krona but these were wholly overcome by an extremely unusual advertising campaign. Very rapid trial was achieved and consumers identified advertising as their prime motivation. Subsequent research showed that the advertising had become an important element in the continuing satisfaction provided by Krona to its users.

BUSINESS BACKGROUND

The Yellow Fats Market

Krona operates within the Yellow Fats Market, which comprises butter, margarine and low fat spreads.

This is a huge market worth £600m at RSP in 1979, but it is not showing many signs of real growth. Indeed, it has declined by about one per cent since 1975.

Within this total picture there have been major shifts in the consumption of butter and margarine. A number of factors are at work here. After the war and with the ending of rationing, consumers switched back to butter in a big way, a trend which reached its peak in the 1960s (although per capita consumption never reached the prewar level). Since then the picture has gradually been reversed so that, by the end of 1979, butter and margarine shared the market equally. The trend to margarine has continued strongly in 1980.

The reasons for this are partly the major improvements in the quality of margarine, in particular the development of soft margarine in tubs, partly the development of specialist margarines and low fat spreads designed to tap concerns about health and diet but, most of all, changes in relative price.

Movements in relative price are quite clearly the dominant influence on sector shares of the Yellow Fats Market. Since a period of roughly level-pegging in the early 1970s, the rate of increase of butter prices has been significantly ahead of that of margarine. Because butter does not operate in a free market but is subject to import quotas and subsidies the precise movement of prices is difficult to predict, but all forecasts assume that a substantial premium for butter over margarine will remain.

Van den Berghs in the Market

Van den Berghs are the leading manufacturers in the market with a share well in excess of 50 per cent. They have the long established brand leader in Stork and have pioneered most of the major technical developments both in soft margarine – with Blue Band – and in opening up the specialist sectors with Flora and Outline.

With a substantial share of the market already, Van den Berghs see the best prospects for profit growth as being, therefore, the further development of the more profitable premium brands but, more importantly, increasing the size of the total sector by maximizing gains from butter.

Market Opportunity

The motivation and mechanism of the move to margarine from butter can vary. The major reason will inevitably be economy and any brand priced below butter may benefit. But there are other triggers too. The softness and ease of spreading of tub margarines are attractive to housewives who have a lot of spreading to do and in cookery too. In some families the taste of margarine becomes preferred to that of butter. The health and slimming claims of Flora and Outline obviously work on certain minority sections of butter users.

But the inescapable common element of all these examples is the fact that butter users are moving – indeed, until Krona, are forced to move – to very different products, which match neither the physical characteristics, the taste, nor the texture of butter. Now while, as explained above, this may be the precise reason for the move for some consumers, it does leave unsatisfied that large potential group of consumers who find the increasing price of butter a problem but are unwilling to sacrifice what they see as the unique qualities of butter. So as the price gap widened, a major opportunity was seen to exist for a margarine which duplicated the characteristics of butter but at a significantly lower price.

The search for a genuine butter substitute is not new. For many years Stork claimed to be indistinguishable from butter and, while arguably falling short of this in practice, was built to brand leader. More recently, Unigate launched St Ivel Gold: not strictly a margarine but a mixture of butter and vegetable oils offering a close-to-butter taste and texture. But it came in semi-soft form in a tub, did not have a generally acceptable taste and was limited to use as a spread. So there existed both a technical problem in making an acceptable product and a considerable credibility problem in persuading consumers that such a product could exist.

The margarine that raised questions in an Australian parliament.

In Sydney Australia, several years ago, an extraordinary rumour started amongst housewives.

It grew to such proportions that the New South Wales Government became involved. And it all began over something as simple as a margarine.

So successful did this margarine become, that housewives were even buying it by the caseful. People were taking it off lorries when it was delivered at supermarkets, to be certain of buying some.

All this activity led to the Minister of Agriculture being asked questions about the product in parliament.

For the rumour was that it wasn't margarine at all. Its taste was that good.

The counterpart of this Australian Margarine is on sale in Britain.

It's called Krona.

Area Choice

Westward and Harlech (82 per cent Test Market Area) were selected for the launch of Krona for the following reasons:

1. Approximately 10 per cent of the UK would be covered – a sample judged to be large enough to assist in network forecasting, yet small enough to minimize capital investment.
2. The area was strong for butter and relatively poor for all margarine. If Krona achieved target, then it was likely to be successful elsewhere.
3. The area is strong for sweet cream (salted) as opposed to lactic (unsalted) butter.
4. St Ivel Gold had begun testing in the same region – consumer acceptance of the two new yellow fat concepts (Krona, a butter grade margarine; St Ivel Gold, a butter/margarine spread) could therefore easily be monitored.
5. The area is strong for packet margarine: it therefore provided the best opportunity to assess whether housewives would perceive Krona as a conventional packet margarine or a butter substitute.

Media Group Selection

Television was the most appropriate medium for announcing Krona. Its various advantages, in combination, were judged to outweigh the disadvantages associated with its sole use:

1. It was felt that the recommended creative approach would be less effective in any other medium.
2. High coverage of the broad target audience of all housewives could be attained (90 per cent).
3. Fast coverage could be achieved.
4. Television is intrusive: important when advertising a basic commodity.
5. Other media groups could not supply appropriate regional test market facilities (unsatisfactory coverage and/or high cost).
6. Test market discounts offered by ITV contractors are helpful.
7. Television advertising tends to be seen by the retail trade as a confident sign of marketing intention.
8. The facility to upweight advertising at short notice was a plus point.

The disadvantage associated with television is that of inadequate coverage/frequency against the light- and non-ITV housewife viewing group. Figures suggested that housewives responsible for a sizeable proportion of total butter and margarine consumption would receive a disproportionately low measure of advertising weight.

    The problem was noted, but the recommendation for the solus use of television remained for the launch year. Additional media in the test area would have to be funded from the (National Equivalent) budget, and this would have meant a disproportionate reduction in weight for the preferred medium. It was proposed that a secondary medium, press, would be employed once relatively low weight ITV continuation bursts were bought in Year 2.

Rate of Strike

The theoretical budget would buy approximately 2400 TVR (45 seconds) during the launch year. High and rapid awareness of the new product amongst housewives was considered to be vital to the success of the brand.

It was therefore proposed that the ratings be deployed in short bursts rather than spread over a longer period at a much reduced rate of strike. The launch burst target was set at 1000 H/W TVRs over four weeks to minimize the coverage problems associated with light- and non-ITV viewers and achieve adequate exposure of the three launch commercials.

CAMPAIGN EVALUATION

Brand Performance

DELIVERIES

Despite two major interruptions, Krona deliveries during the first twelve months exceeded expectations and by the end of the period were running at four to five times initial levels.

The pattern was affected by two industrial disputes, the lorry drivers' strike (2nd January to 5th February 1979) and a dispute at Van den Berghs' Bromborough factory. The former sharply reduced deliveries in cycles 1 and 2 1979 while the latter meant that there were no deliveries of Krona (or of other of Van den Berghs' brands) between the beginning of April and the beginning of May 1979.

The resumption of deliveries after the strike was not uniform across all Van den Berghs' brands and Krona received priority. This, to a degree, explains a peak in deliveries in cycles 12 and 13 1979. However, this was not, as might have been expected, a temporary phenomenon and Krona sales were established at a new high level up to cycle 20.

Overall, the figures show a pipe-line filling phase at the end of 1978, a confused period in the first quarter of 1979, a further pipe-line filling phase in cycle 11 but then evidence of very substantial sales when normal deliveries could be resumed.

DISTRIBUTION

Figures are available only for sterling weighted distribution in the two areas combined, in Multiples and Co-ops only (Table 1.1).

Very strong distribution was thus achieved within two or three months and growth in distribution cannot fully explain the growth in deliveries.

TABLE 1.1: KRONA STERLING DISTRIBUTION, HARLECH AND WESTWARD

October/November 1978	78%
December 1978/January 1979	95%
February/March	95%
April/May	89%
June/July	95%
August/September	86%
October/November	93%

Stats MR.

CONSUMER SALES/SHARE

Within three TCA periods, Krona had achieved a 10 per cent share, making it Number 2 brand in the market (Table 1.2).

TABLE 1.2: KRONA VOLUME BRAND SHARE

1978						4 w/e:		1979				
14/10	11/11	9/12	6/1	3/2	3/3	31/3	28/4	26/5	23/6	21/7	18/8	15/9
–	5	10	9	5	8	12	5	3	14	15	18	16

TCA.

This was a time of rapid sampling. Cumulative penetration had reached 24 per cent by November (see below).

There was a temporary set-back as a result of the lorry drivers strike but share recovered strongly by March, only to be hit again by the Van den Berghs strike. As explained earlier, Krona benefited by a shortage of other Van den Berghs brands in June, but, far from falling back when normal supplies were resumed, it actually made large volume gains in subsequent periods. By the end of the first twelve months, Krona was brand leader, with around twice the share of the next brand.

The Consumer

AWARENESS

The first post-check showed that awareness after only five weeks of advertising had already reached a high level and this was then maintained in subsequent months despite the interruptions in supply caused by strikes early in 1979. Considering the very substantial brand shares achieved, the level of spontaneous awareness could seem on the low side. However, viewed in the context of the lowish figures for long established brands such as Stork and Blue Band, Krona's achievement may be judged satisfactory. Certainly prompted awareness was at a very high level for a new brand (Table 1.3).

TABLE 1.3: KRONA AWARENESS (SPONTANEOUS/PROMPTED)

November	February	July/August
20/79	22/86	25/80

Quick Read

TRIAL

To be tried by one quarter of all housewives within little more than a month was obviously an exceptional achievement and the brand continued to gain trial in the succeeding months (Table 1.4).

TABLE 1.4: KRONA TRIAL (% BOUGHT IN LAST SIX MONTHS)

November	February	July/August
24%	38%	43%

Quick Read.

Obviously, the advertising cannot take sole credit for initial trial. A door-to-door coupon was dropped during October and there were a number of in-store demonstrations. By the end of 1978, distribution in Multiples and Co-ops exceeded 90 per cent sterling. However, there is good evidence that advertising played a major role:

INFLUENCES ON FIRST PURCHASE

The November Quick Read Survey showed:

Coupon received or not

No. of respondents aware of Krona:	248
Yes	47%
No	50%
Don't know, etc.	3%

Whether coupon first encouraged trial

No. of respondents	44
Yes	34%
No	66%
Don't know, etc.	–

Awareness of Krona TV advertising

No. of respondents aware of Krona:	248
Yes	91%
No	7%
Don't know, etc.	2%

A separate survey was carried out at the end of November 1978 among Krona buyers in the two areas:

Source of awareness of Krona

No. ever bought	186
TV advertising	66%
Leaflet/Coupon	13%
Friend told me	13%
In-Store	11%

Seen Krona advertised on TV

No. not mentioning TV above	63
Yes	68%
No	17%
Don't know	14%

Combined with those mentioning TV previously this gives a total of 89 per cent who claimed to have seen Krona advertising on TV, while only a small percentage related their awareness of Krona to the coupon.

Similar information was sought in the March/April Taylor Nelson Survey. This showed that among trialists a majority of both acceptors (59 per cent) and rejectors (63 per cent) gave TV advertising as the main reason for trying Krona in the first place. Obviously, by this time, some while had elapsed since the coupon drop, while there had been a substantial weight of TV advertising, but at the very least it demonstrates the importance advertising was seen to have as a source of information on the brand.

This information should be seen against the context of the general reluctance of consumers to admit advertising as an influence on their behaviour.

REPEAT PURCHASE

The Quick Read Monitors show a steady increase in the numbers of housewives intending to purchase Krona next time (17 per cent of respondents by July/August). By July/August, more than two thirds of buyers had bought more than one pack. Obviously the recruitment rate of new users shows a sharp drop over the period of the surveys, although sampling was still going on. As long after the launch as July/August 1979, over one third of housewives who had ever bought Krona had bought Krona as their last purchase. The November 1978 Krona Buyers' Survey confirmed that, within not much more than a month, 50 to 60 per cent of buyers had bought more than one pack.

The March Taylor Nelson Survey showed that 50 per cent of buyers said that they would definitely buy again and a further 29 per cent would probably buy again. Outright rejection was at a minimal level. Over two thirds of buyers had at that point bought more than one pack.

PRODUCT POSITIONING

The aim of Krona advertising was to present the brand as a high quality spreading margarine, indistinguishable from butter. Was this being borne out in practice in the market-place?

The November 1978 Buyers' Survey indicated that even in the earliest stage of the brand's life, when sampling was at its peak, around half of current Krona buyers felt they had stopped buying other brands or cut down on them. In each case the largest single source of Krona business was butter.

The March 1979 Taylor Nelson Study confirmed this picture, around half acceptors and a quarter of rejectors who had substituted Krona for another product having switched from butter.

Switching from other margarine brands at this point did not show any clear pattern, but certainly there was no demonstrable association of Krona with cheap packet cooking margarine.

HOW THE ADVERTISING WORKS

The brand, then, in its first twelve months in the two areas was clearly highly successful in sales and share terms. A high level of trial had been achieved in a short period and the brand had largely been received by consumers in the way intended. It had lived up to or exceeded expectation for a substantial body of consumers and good levels of repeat purchase were achieved.

Advertising had been identified by consumers as the primary influence on their initial purchase and this is confirmed by the most sensible interpretation of the sales and attitude data discussed.

A fair amount of evidence exists to explain how the Krona launch campaign works.

Sources

We derive our understanding of how the advertising works, as opposed to the influences it has on purchasing behaviour, from several sources:

(a) The various quantitative surveys already quoted.
(b) Qualitative research into the finished commercials prior to transmission and two qualitative studies carried out to assist creative development.

Communication

Our analysis can be divided into two sections: communication and persuasion.

We know from a lot of past research that the concept of a margarine identical to butter (and at a lower price) is highly appealing.

The problem, as we discussed earlier, is to overcome the hurdles provided by restrictive regulation and credibility and communicate the concept effectively and persuasively.

It is clear from the evidence that the communication was understood. In the qualitative studies the main message was seen as:

'It's as good as butter'
'Closer to butter than other margarines'
'Tastes more like butter'
'Alternative to butter'
'Implying it was as good as butter'

The March Taylor Nelson Study showed that over half of acceptors and 42 per cent of rejectors expected either a new brand of butter or something similar.

Persuasion

In terms of persuasion, we have the evidence of image statements from the various Quick Read Studies. These show that:

(a) Despite the legacy of incredibility and the current status of packet margarines, communication *and* persuasion that Krona was a high quality margarine with a butter-like taste was well achieved.
(b) Levels of agreement were high, even in November 1978 *when a substantial majority had only the evidence of the advertising to go on.*

Not surprisingly, acceptance or otherwise of this message became a touchstone of trial of Krona and subsequent repurchase, and in research carried out after the launch there is a substantial division on this issue between acceptors and rejectors.

The advertising had clearly established the pretensions of Krona. It was up to the brand itself to live up to the claims or not.

How was persuasion achieved to the point of trial? The following interpretation is a distillation of the findings of the various qualitative studies mentioned earlier:

STYLE AND TONE

The novel 'documentary' style of the commercials was liked because:

(i) It was different from other, particularly margarine, advertisements.
(ii) The tone was 'telling not selling'. It left the choice to the consumer; it treated her as an adult; it did not talk down to her. The personality of René Cutforth was important here.
(iii) The tone was serious and gave stature to the product.

All combined strongly to enhance credibility.

LOCATION

The Australian context worked in a number of ways:

(i) It was interesting and different.
(ii) It took Krona out of the conventional margarine context.
(iii) It had definite 'dairy' connotations.
(iv) It was related to the UK, though not part of it.
(v) It was a desirable place to be – redolent not so much of affluence, but of a good, healthy, open-air life.

Trial and Repeat Purchase

Finally, the evidence suggested that the campaign was trial *and* repeat purchase orientated. While for some people it clearly on its own could not overcome rooted scepticism about margarine claims, for the majority it provided a strong inducement to try. Once people had tried and accepted the product, the advertising was seen as a confirmation of their experience. They too had made this discovery. They too could not believe it was a margarine. What had happened in Australia was only to be expected. In addition, the intelligent tone of the commercials complimented them as consumers and confirmed the good sense of their choice of Krona. It is quite reasonable on the evidence, then, to claim that the Krona advertising, far from simply conveying a highly desirable message, has by its distinctive character become an essential part of the brand's character and therefore a crucial element in the success of this very major grocery brand.

CONCLUSION

That Krona represented a major marketing success in Harlech and Westward over the period under review is amply demonstrated by the facts. Nor was it a temporary phenomenon. Krona is achieving similar results in other areas as it is extended and has more than maintained its dominance in its original test areas.

We say 'marketing success' deliberately because, as we all know, the successful launch of a new product depends on many related factors. In the case of Krona these were:

1. TIMING

The increasing price premium of butter over margarine provided the opportunity for a brand aimed at people forced to trade down.

2. PRODUCT QUALITY

Krona was the first margarine successfully to simulate butter. It exceeds expectations and arouses almost a religious fervour among converts.

3. NAMING AND PACKAGING

The presentation of the brand communicates the required positioning and reinforces the belief of users that Krona is closer to butter than margarine.

4. PRICING

While Krona is clearly a premium-priced margarine, it is sufficiently cheaper than butter to make the incentive to switch as strong as possible.

5. MARKETING INVESTMENT

Van den Berghs recognized the potential of the brand and were prepared to spend heavily behind it, above and below the line, in its first year. Significantly, the bulk of this money was spent on the consumer in order to encourage the critically important first purchase and not to reduce price at point-of-sale.

6. ADVERTISING

Because of these factors it would be easy to argue that almost any advertising would have worked for Krona. This is not the case, for these reasons:

1. The problem in persuading housewives to accept Krona was formidable. Conventionally, packet margarines were cheap cooking media. Yet here was a premium-priced brand. Previous claims of butter-parity had proved to be excessive. Yet here was a brand ringing the same bell again. Regulations forbade explicit or implicit comparisons with butter, yet here was a brand whose whole raison d'être was that it was indistinguishable from butter.

    Krona achieved not only very rapid and high awareness, which could be put down to the substantial TV expenditure, but rapid trial too.

    While hard evidence of precise cause and effect is unavailable and indeed unattainable to apportion credit between advertising, coupon drop and POS, the view of housewives expressed repeatedly in quantitative and qualitative studies puts advertising as the major influence.

2. Krona's role is to be a cheap substitute for butter. Knowing the strong emotional aura surrounding butter, this role is one which legitimately might be expected to reach the housewife's pocket, but not her heart. In fact there is growing evidence that Krona is on the way to becoming a 'religion' for its users. There is a sense of a 'miracle', that the housewife has made 'a discovery' which she wants to pass on to others.

There is no doubt that the advertising, with its serious and intelligent tone and the story which it tells, is contributing importantly to this.

APPENDIX: DATA USED IN KRONA ADVERTISING EVALUATION

Sales

1. Van den Bergh delivery figures
2. TCA
3. Stats MR Distribution Check: Multiples and Co-ops

Consumer

QUICK READ MONITORS

A series of quantitative studies based on the Quick Reading method developed by Unilever Marketing Division was carried out.

    Research was among margarine users (who form around 80 per cent of the population) in Harlech and Westward, quota-ed by age and class.

KRONA BUYERS' SURVEY

187 housewives who had ever bought Krona were interviewed in-home in Harlech (95) and Westward (92). Interviewing was conducted between 27th November and 1st December 1978.

KRONA MARKET MONITOR: HARLECH AND WESTWARD (TAYLOR NELSON & ASSOCIATES) MARCH/ APRIL 1979

Main Objectives:

1. Evaluate Krona's success in terms of awareness and penetration.
2. Investigate Krona's future in terms of likelihood of repurchase or trial (non-users).
3. Evaluate effects of experience on perceived product acceptability and positioning.

Method:

Area: Harlech and Westward TV areas.
Sample: Based on contact interviews with a quota sample of 945 housewives, three subsamples were identified, who were taken through an extended interview:

(a) Respondents who had bought Krona and would definitely or probably buy again in the future (acceptors).
(b) Respondents who had bought Krona but did not know or were unlikely to buy again in the future (rejectors).
(c) Respondents who were aware of Krona and had seen a pack in-store (aware non-buyers).

QUALITATIVE RESEARCH: QUICKSEARCH 1979

30 individual interviews: 15 trialists who either had Krona at home at the time of interview or would have had it if it were available. 15 non-trialists. All aware of Krona advertising with a spread by weight of ITV viewing.

Objectives:

(a) To evaluate response to the launch campaign after four months' exposure.
(b) To elicit response to a possible follow-up campaign.

QUALITATIVE RESEARCH: GREGORY LANGMAID ASSOCIATES (MARCH 1979)

This research consisted of four groups and 16 depth interviews in Swansea and Bristol. All respondents were from the BC1C2 social grades, aged between 20 and 55.
   Half were users (bought twice or more) of Krona, half were non-users and non-rejectors of the brand. These latter were women who had heard of Krona but who had not bought or tried it.

Objectives:

(a) To examine attitudes to Krona in the test market area among users and non-users as a background to exploring the acceptability and comprehension of two new Krona commercials in terms of their effects on users and non-users.
(b) To examine the continuity of the new films leading on from the earlier Australian films.
(c) To probe the suitability and effectiveness of René Cutforth as a presenter.

2

The Case for All Clear Shampoo

BACKGROUND

Introduction

The anti-dandruff shampoo market is a considerable part of the total shampoo market with the medicated shampoo sector constituting some 35 per cent in 1979 of the total value of the market. It is dominated by Procter and Gamble's Head & Shoulders – brand leader of the entire shampoo markets of both the UK and USA.

In 1978 Elida Gibbs found itself well established in most segments of the shampoo market, but it lacked proper representation in the anti-dandruff shampoo sector.

Market research carried out by Elida had nonetheless revealed a market opportunity not yet exploited by Procter and Gamble. The evidence showed that there was a need for a range of anti-dandruff shampoos for different hair conditions, that is, an anti-dandruff shampoo for greasy hair, one for dry hair, and one for normal hair.

Elida Gibbs developed this range under the brand name All Clear. It was test-marketed for a year in the Southern area. This was successful and Elida Gibbs launched their new anti-dandruff range of shampoos nationally in July 1979.

Marketing and Advertising Objectives

The marketing objective was to gain a significant share of the shampoo market by positioning ourselves in the anti-dandruff segment of the market.

The shampoo market is highly fragmented and very competitive and it was judged that a volume brand share in excess of 5 per cent would be a considerable achievement.

The advertising objectives were:
  (i) to announce All Clear as a new brand in the anti-dandruff shampoo sector;
 (ii) to communicate the unique features of All Clear, namely, that it had a range of three variants, each suitable for a particular hair type: clears dandruff and cares for hair;
(iii) to position All Clear as a shampoo suitable for men and women.

Description of the Campaign

The launch was scheduled to begin in July 1979 with national TV advertising. Two TV commercials were made, one targeted at the female audience, the other at the male audience. Both commercials lasted 30 seconds.

The ITV strike which occurred a few weeks after the beginning of the launch necessitated a change in the original media plan. The campaign was redirected into press and radio. Only after the strike, in January 1980, did All Clear get the TV support which, it was believed, it needed.

The Period of Time under Consideration

This paper addresses itself to the period of time from the national launch of All Clear in July 1979 to March 1980.

CAMPAIGN EVALUATION

Although the ITV strike coincided with the launch of All Clear, it does enable us to review the effectiveness of the different media employed in the All Clear campaign, and to gauge the importance of television advertising to this brand.

The Methodology of Evaluation

To evaluate the effectiveness of the advertising, it has been necessary to analyse the effect of the individual component parts of the marketing mix and other contiguous factors, for example, competitive advertising activity. This is done below and from it, by a process of elimination, our conclusion is that the TV advertising campaign which started in January 1980 was the single most important influence in the success of the All Clear launch.

The Effect of Pricing

Variations in the sizes of bottles of shampoo make it necessary to convert actual prices to £s per litre of shampoo for comparability between brands. From these figures an index has been constructed to provide a measure of the price advantage which All Clear held over Head & Shoulders during the period under examination. Table 2.1 below shows this index, where 100 would equal price parity with Head & Shoulders, anything less than 100 therefore equalling a price advantage for All Clear.

TABLE 2.1: INDEX OF THE RELATIVE PRICE ADVANTAGE OF ALL CLEAR OVER HEAD & SHOULDERS

	1979 July	Aug	Sept	Oct	Nov	Dec	1980 Jan	Feb	Mar
100 = price parity with Head & Shoulders	68	71	72	82	79	82	87	88	90

This index shows that All Clear's price *increased* throughout the period under examination. The price of Head & Shoulders also increased, but at a slower rate than that of All Clear, so that All Clear's price advantage over Head & Shoulders *decreased* during this period.

January and February saw All Clear's price advantage at its then lowest, but Table 2.2 shows that it was these months which saw its brand share at its highest.

The absence of any correlation between price advantage and brand share is clearly demonstrated when volume brand share and the index of relative price advantage (see Table 2.3) are seen together.

Stills from All Clear television advertisement: 'Trouble is, the dandruff keeps coming back.'

TABLE 2.2: STERLING BRAND SHARES OF ALL CLEAR AND HEAD & SHOULDERS

| | 1979 | | | | | | 1980 | | |
	July %	*Aug* %	*Sept* %	*Oct* %	*Nov* %	*Dec* %	*Jan* %	*Feb* %	*Mar* %
All Clear	5	7	5	5	6	4	8	8	6
Head & Shoulders	14	13	13	13	13	11	13	16	15

TCPI.

TABLE 2.3: VOLUME BRAND SHARE AND INDEX OF RELATIVE PRICE ADVANTAGE FOR ALL CLEAR

| | 1979 | | | | | | 1980 | | |
	Jul	*Aug*	*Sept*	*Oct*	*Nov*	*Dec*	*Jan*	*Feb*	*Mar*
% volume brand share (litres)	4	6	4	4	4	3	6	6	4
Index of price advantage	68	71	72	82	79	82	87	88	90

'So it cares for my kind of hair and it really clears my dandruff ...'

The Effect of Consumer Promotions

In measuring the relative pricing of All Clear against Head & Shoulders, price was calculated by dividing volume into a value figure derived from purchases at *actual* prices. By this method all money-off consumer promotions have already been accounted for.

The only consumer promotion which did not involve a 'money-off' offer, a competition, ran in October and November 1979. Its closing date was 31st December 1979. The competition involved a leaflet drop to 10 million households, with cash prizes for the winners.

The objective of this consumer promotion was less to stimulate consumer purchase than

TABLE 2.4: PERCENTAGE VOLUME BRAND SHARE (LITRES)

	1979 Jul %	Aug %	Sept %	Oct %	Nov %	Dec %	1980 Jan %	Feb %	Mar %
All Clear	4	6	4	4	4	3	6	6	4
Head & Shoulders	9	8	8	8	8	7	8	11	10
Total medicated	26	29	27	28	27	26	29	31	29

'New All Clear: clears dandruff, cares for hair.'

to increase both consumer and trade awareness of, and interest in, All Clear. The consumer promotion was linked to a trade promotion (see below).

This consumer promotion had little effect on the October–December consumer sales as is shown by volume brand share figures in Table 2.4.

The Effect of Trade Promotions and Distribution

Most of the trade promotional activity, specifically trade discounts, took place very early in the launch programme to obtain shelf-facings and listings with the major Multiples.

The consumer promotion described above was linked to a trade promotion with the aim of increasing awareness and interest in All Clear. The trade promotion, which took the form of a lottery, preceded the consumer promotion and its closing date was 6th November 1979.

TABLE 2.5: INDEX OF QUARTERLY STERLING DISTRIBUTION FOR ALL CLEAR
IN CHEMISTS AND GROCERS

	July 1979	November 1979	January 1980	March 1980
Grocers	100	130	117	137
Chemists	100	128	134	132

The effect of this promotion would have been reflected in the November and December distribution figures. Table 2.5 shows the quarterly distribution figures for All Clear in chemists and grocers indexed to a base of 100 for July 1979.

As Table 2.5 illustrates, distribution figures did show an increase in November over July 1979, although in grocery outlets distribution started to decline in January. Increasing distribution through to January in the chemists was probably a reflection of their usual increases in stocking at this time to meet the annual increase in consumer purchases of shampoos immediately after Christmas.

Increased distribution in November in both chemists and grocers did not, however, lead to any significant increase in consumer purchase in November and December. Table 2.6 below shows All Clear's performance in absolute volume terms indexed to 100 in July 1979.

TABLE 2.6: INDEX OF ALL CLEAR'S ABSOLUTE VOLUME PERFORMANCE (LITRES)

| | 1979 | | | | | | 1980 | | |
	Jul	Aug	Sept	Oct	Nov	Dec	Jan	Feb	Mar
	100	128	95	95	97	63	140	115	93

The Product

The product and range remained exactly the same throughout the period under examination. A new 50 ml sized bottle was introduced at the end of February 1980, but distribution was not complete until the end of March. This introduction therefore had no significant influence on performance during the months under consideration.

Competitive Activity

The shampoo market in general is both fragmented (with over 35 advertised brands listed in MEAL over the past two years) and highly competitive with significant levels of advertising expenditure on major brands.

All Clear's media split (based on MEAL figures) for the months under consideration is shown in Table 2.7 below.

So as to assess how much 'interference' there might have been from other shampoo brands advertising at this time, it is useful to look at All Clear's media expenditure in terms of its 'share' of total shampoo advertising expenditure, its 'share of the media voice'. Table 2.8 details All Clear's 'share of voice' and compares it with that achieved by Head & Shoulders.

The 'share of voice' figures show that All Clear achieved its most significant shares of

TABLE 2.7: MEDIA SPLIT FOR ALL CLEAR (£'000s)

| | 1979 | | | | | | 1980 | | |
	Jul	Aug	Sept	Oct	Nov	Dec	Jan	Feb	Mar
TV	116	29	–	–	–	–	266	59	–
Press	–	–	74	86	72	–	–	3	–
Radio	–	–	–	52	52	–	–	–	–
Total	116	29	74	138	124	–	266	62	–

TABLE 2.8: 'SHARE OF VOICE' FOR ALL CLEAR AND HEAD & SHOULDERS

	1979 Jul %	Aug %	Sept %	Oct %	Nov %	Dec %	1980 Jan %	Feb %	Mar %
All Clear	9	7	33	21	12	–	38	12	–
Head & Shoulders	14	15	–	27	25	44	17	17	22

MEAL.

advertising expenditure in September 1979 and January 1980. The high share in September is largely due to the absence of spending by Head & Shoulders, but this high share did not result in high brand share (see Table 2.2).

The Relationship between Brand Share and Television Advertising

The highest 'share of voice' of advertising expenditure was in fact in January (38 per cent),

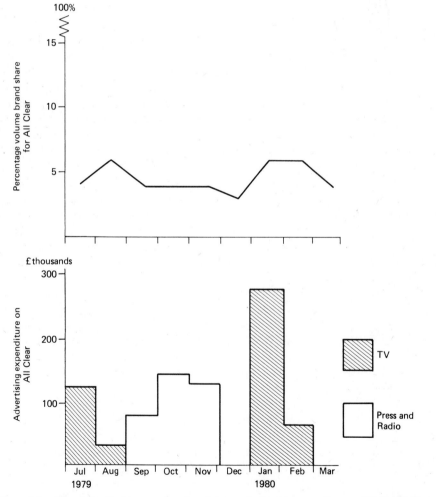

Figure 2.1. *The relationship between volume brand share and advertising expenditure on TV for All Clear.*

the month which did see a dramatic rise in volume share from 3 per cent in December to 6 per cent in January.

It is our contention that brand share doubled in January not only because of the amount of money spent on advertising, but also because the advertising medium had reverted to TV.

Further evidence that television has been the most effective medium for All Clear is that its television spend of £116 000 in late July was reflected in the August volume brand share of 6 per cent. This share dropped immediately to 4 per cent when the ITV strike prevented further advertising on television. All Clear did not regain its 6 per cent volume share until the resumption of commercial television and its advertising in that medium in January 1980.

The clear relationship between All Clear's volume brand share and television advertising is illustrated in Figure 2.1.

THE SIZE OF THE EFFECT

The Effect of Television vs. the Effect of Radio and Press

The £262 000 spent on radio and press advertising in October and November generated £624 000 (according to TCPI) in consumer purchases over the three-month period of October to December.

The £325 000 spent on television advertising in January and February generated £972 000 in consumer purchases in the period January to March.

Thus it may be said that a marginal increase of £63 000 in advertising expenditure (from £262 000 to £325 000) and a change from radio and press to television generated an additional £348 000 (£972 000 − £624 000) in consumer purchases.

Whilst the three months, October to December, in total may be considered 'average' for the year, there is a cyclical annual increase in shampoo sales after Christmas (which between 1979 and 1980 increased by approximately 20 per cent). To take this annual increase into account, 20 per cent is deducted from the January to March figure to give a truer picture of the effectiveness of television advertising.

Thus for a marginal increase of £63 000 and a change to television advertising, a further £278 000 of consumer purchases were generated than would have been had radio and press expenditure continued through to January and February.

To summarize:

	Consumer purchases £	Advertising expenditure £
Jan/Mar 1980	972 000	325 000
Oct/Dec 1979	624 000	262 000
Gross increase	348 000	63 000
Deduct 20% for seasonal increases	70 000	
Net increases	278 000	63 000

The Opportunity Cost of not Advertising at all in January and February

The two months, December and March, in which there was no advertising expenditure are marked in both instances by a fall in value brand share (to 3 per cent in December and 4 per cent in March).

Assuming, then, that a value brand share of 4 per cent represents an achievable brand share without any advertising, the following revenue would have been generated for All Clear in the first three months of 1980:

January	£185 120
February	£172 920
March	£172 240
Total	£530 280

Adding the actual advertising expenditure for January and February to the above, we get a truer picture of Elida Gibbs' potential position without advertising:

Sales	£530 280
Savings on advertising	£325 000
	£855 280

The opportunity cost of not advertising, therefore, is the actual revenue less the potential without advertising:

	£972 000
less	£855 280
	£116 720

Thus the size of the effect of television advertising may be represented by the difference between the actual and potential revenue. Had Elida Gibbs not advertised to the extent they did on television in January and February, they would have lost nearly £117 000 in revenue from consumer purchases (during the first three months of 1980).

3
Whitegates

A Regional Success Story

INTRODUCTION

This paper concerns the launch of not only a new service, but also a new company – a new company in a traditional consumer service sector.

Although to date it can only be presented and titled as 'A Regional Success Story', it is, nevertheless, a case history in which the role of advertising has played a vital, practical and major role. Furthermore, it is the author's contention that, although the level of success which has been achieved is only in a geographically restricted marketing region, this does not in any way diminish the importance of the advertising effectiveness element. The claimed level of success will be demonstrated, as will the part that advertising has played.

Because the submission deals with a 'new service' rather than goods, the measurement criteria cannot be based simply on the 'hard' measurement of sales, but must, of necessity, be based on the equally significant and (in this case) more relevant measurements of behavioural evidence, attitudes and awareness as well as on the sheer growth and success record of the new company. The reason for using these measurement criteria will become obvious in later sections.

The effectiveness of the strategy and campaign involved and the level of marketing achievement can be summarized as follows:

In less than two and a half years, the campaign concerned has successfully launched an entirely new company offering a dramatically different service in a traditionally competitive field of consumer service. It has done so through an aggressive and effective advertising campaign supported by other important elements of the marketing mix to the point where the company concerned can now claim market leadership in the area with a record of growth and expansion far in excess of the most optimistic forecasts.

Whilst it is, overall, a marketing success, the part that advertising has played is recognized as, and agreed to be, enormous. Without the solid foundation stones of truly effective advertising, such a marketing success could not have been built.

BACKGROUND

Provident Financial Group Limited, based in Bradford, is a public company specializing in consumer credit – the largest consumer credit trading organization of its kind. Through a number of subsidiary companies, Provident Personal Credit, Practical Credit Services, etc., the Group provides consumer credit to the weekly paid market and principally serves C2D households. The Group has, for a number of years, been considering areas for diversification and opportunity. The main criteria, in consideration of diversifying markets, were to employ the skills and facilities possessed by the Group. These were identified as in-depth management and marketing skills, finance, and the availability of computer capacity and expertise (the Group has its own massive computer complex designed to service the multiple transactions involved through its various credit trading organizations).

The corporate planning unit within the Group had identified various markets which could make use of these resources and facilities and in 1977 the decision was taken to apply the availability of computer capacity and techniques, linked to management and finance, to enter the field of domestic property estate agency. In-depth research of the domestic estate agency market throughout the United Kingdom and the real estate market in the United States led the company to the conclusion that the concept of using computer time and skills in house marketing presented an opportunity in the United Kingdom.

Consequently, in mid-1977, it was decided to launch, in one region of the country, an entirely new estate agency concept. The new service using the house marketing idea would utilize the computer's capability to match buyers with sellers through a central matching facility. It would also offer a comprehensive computer-backed service featuring fixed fees, a 'no-sale, no-charge' agreement, seven days a week opening, evening opening hours and the production of a computer compiled *Property Weekly* with a highly efficient computer controlled mailing service.

MARKETING AND ADVERTISING OBJECTIVES

The launch of the new service was planned for 1st January 1978 and a decision was taken to promote the completely new house marketing (estate agency) service in the Yorkshire television region.

Desk research showed that Yorkshire represented an area typical of the UK market with profiles of home ownership, households and individuals very much in line with the rest of the country (Tables 3.1, 3.2 and 3.3).

A more precise sample of the United Kingdom could hardly have been obtained. This fact, coupled with the convenience of the area (being the company's home territory, thus

TABLE 3.1: TYPE OF TENURE

	GB %	Yorkshire %
Owner occupied	52.5	52.8
buying home	31.3	32.8
own outright	21.2	20.0
Rent from Council	35.1	33.8
Other tenure	12.4	13.4
All adults	100.0	100.0

TGI, 1976.

TABLE 3.2: AGE OF DWELLINGS – DECEMBER 1974

	GB %	Yorkshire %
Pre-1918	33	33
1919–1944	23	23
Post-1944	44	44
Total	100	100

Abstract of Regional Statistics, 1975.

TABLE 3.3: PROFILES OF HOUSEHOLDS IN YORKSHIRE AND UK

	UK 000s	%	Yorkshire 000s	%	Yorkshire % of UK
All households	19 304	100	2524	100	13.1
Social class:					
AB	2316	12	256	10	11.1
C1	3772	20	442	18	11.7
C2	6690	35	967	38	14.5
DE	6526	34	859	34	13.2

making it more easy to monitor and control), made it the most obvious launch area for the venture.

In light of the competitive nature of the market, coupled with the investment needed, and the uncertainty of the level of success, no detailed expansion plans beyond the Yorkshire television area were set down, although outline proposals were made.

The initial plan was to have two offices operational on 1st January 1978 serving the Leeds and Bradford conurbations and it was at this stage that the Group's agency, Bowden Dyble and Hayes Limited, was brought in to help develop the detailed marketing and advertising plans. The agency's initial brief included the need to develop a title and style for the company: the project at this stage was still being referred to as 'House Marketing Limited'. There was a need to establish a visual styling for the new organization and to prepare detailed advertising proposals covering media strategy, creative treatment, company image, promotional plans, etc.

Part of the marketing brief was to extend the new estate agency service as quickly as possible throughout the Yorkshire region. The precise rate of expansion was to be dependent upon the success of the first branches in operation. In turn, the success of the operation would be dependent upon rapid build-up of consumer awareness, the acceptance of the new company in a competitive and crowded market, establishment of the company's main selling points, and volume throughput of sellers and buyers.

By definition, the estate agency market is a finite one. There is very little, if anything, that marketeers can do to expand it. People's decisions to buy and sell domestic property are influenced by pressures other than marketing and advertising and there could be no expectation of any market growth to satisfy the newly-formulated company.

Consequently, it was recognized that any growth and expansion of the new service would be obtainable only by capturing market share from existing and, in most cases, well established competitors in the market.

The principal marketing and advertising objective, therefore, had to be the forceful and effective projection of the new service in order to ensure that a significant slice of the existing market was captured at the expense of those existing companies.

It was agreed at this early stage that the principal market sector was to be medium-priced property in the domestic market, but, recognizing that the service had an appeal to *all* house buyers and sellers, there was no limit placed on potential users – neither a lower nor a higher value of property was excluded.

The marketing objective in terms of the development of outlets was to move as quickly as possible to the position of having an outlet in each of the main centres of population in the Yorkshire/Humberside region based on the population assessment (centres and hinterland) of the key centres. The location of branches was agreed to be in city or town centre locations on the premise that, if the new service was promoted effectively enough, prospective customers would be willing to visit centrally based units, particularly since these would be open during weekday evenings and at weekends.

The main centres of population throughout the Yorkshire TV region were identified and these became the prime targets for extension of the new services, the principal centres being Sheffield, Leeds, Hull, Bradford, Barnsley and Doncaster.

CAMPAIGN STRATEGIES

Before describing the particular media and creative strategies developed, it is important to understand that the agency and the company had first of all to overcome the basic problem of how to launch two new estate agency offices on 1st January with no properties on the books. By definition, an estate agency cannot be trading, and therefore can hardly advertise the fact that it is trading, without having a product to sell, i.e. without having some properties 'on the books'. This problem was overcome, before the first two offices commenced to trade, by running an incentive offer in the relevant evening newspapers covering the Leeds and Bradford conurbations.

The offer had to be simple, effective and dramatic. A plan was developed to undertake to sell the first 100 houses on the new estate agent's books at an all-in price of £100 – a very aggressive and competitive offer. This offer was featured for a number of weeks prior to the official opening of the branches and the resulting response ensured that, on the due date of 1st January, the new service and the new offices could be advertised because they now had a stock of properties to which they could apply the services they were offering.

The basic media strategy employed following the opening announcement offer (which has since been used in similar form to launch the opening of all other offices) was the extensive use of Yorkshire Television.

This media decision was taken for five main reasons: (1) there was a need to establish the name and the service quickly; (2) there was a need to project the new service as a modern and go-ahead organization; (3) a local rate facility on the Yorkshire Television rate card (whilst only two offices were involved) offered an advantageous rate opportunity; (4) promotion of the name and the service in the areas not yet served by local offices, i.e. the rest of the Yorkshire Television area, represented a 'softening-up' of that wider territory; (5) the use of the medium clearly distinguished the new organization from the traditional local and regional estate agency services.

For only £100, we'll sell your house on TV.

In January, a new kind of estate agent is opening in Bradford.

We're called Whitegates.

And like one or two of the larger estate agents, we'll be publishing a free property weekly carrying details of all our houses.

But what makes us really different is that the Whitegates Weekly will be advertised regularly and frequently on TV, to over 5½ million people.

So if you sell through Whitegates, you can be pretty certain anyone looking for a house in Yorkshire is going to get details of your property.

Of course, we'll also display a photograph and a description of your house in our Property Showrooms.

(We're the only ones in the area to open seven days a week.)

And we'll register all the details of your property on a £1m computer, which accurately and automatically

EACH WHITEGATES OFFICE IS LINKED TO A MAIN COMPUTER, SO THAT WE CAN MATCH THE EXACT REQUIREMENTS OF ANY PURCHASER AGAINST EVERY HOUSE ON OUR BOOKS, AND IN SECONDS PROVIDE A LIST OF SUITABLE PROPERTIES.

matches houses to potential purchasers.

But what's more we offer all these services at extremely competitive fees.

£100, plus 1% of the selling price of your house. So on a £12,000 house, you'll pay a total of £220.

There are no further costs (except, of course, VAT), no hidden extras whatsoever, and we operate on a strictly no-sale, no-charge basis.

Compare our charges with those made by other estate agents and we think you'll find there's only one way you can get a better deal if you're selling your house.

And that's by taking advantage of our incredible introductory offer.

We're selling the first 100 houses registered at each office for an all-inclusive fee of only £100. It doesn't matter whether your property is priced at £5,000 or £50,000.

To register your house, 'phone the number below, now.

And from January onwards, we'll be selling it on TV.

*Charges and conditions are based on the understanding that Whitegates are appointed on a 'sole agency' basis.

SELLING PRICE	WHITEGATES ALL-INCLUSIVE FEE
£5,000	£150
£10,000	£200
£15,000	£250
£20,000	£300
£25,000	£350

DON'T FORGET, FOR THE WHITEGATES INTRODUCTORY OFFER, YOU'LL STILL SEND OUR STANDARD TERMS CAN SAVE YOU A LOT OF MONEY.

Whitegates

Tomorrow's kind of estate agent.

BRADFORD (0274) 306611

Whitegates press advertisement.

Stills from Whitegates television advertisement.

It was clear from the outset that the new concept of 'house marketing' required a dramatic and modern creative strategy yet still needed to be presented as relevant to the house buying/selling market.

The first creative problem which had to be overcome was the development of a suitable name and styling. Since time was of the essence, the selection of a name had to be made quickly.

Provident Financial Group Limited has many subsidiary and associated companies and there was obviously going to be some advantage, not least from a timing point of view, if an existing registered name could be adopted. One of the Group's registered but inactive companies was Whitegates Finance Limited, and after deliberation it was agreed that the name 'Whitegates' could be made to work in the 'house marketing' market.

The company was therefore registered and developed as 'Whitegates Estate Agency Ltd and the white gate itself became a clear, simple but memorable logo for use in all advertising and promotional elements. The choice of a 'mon repos' gate was deliberate to enable the mass of the house buying/selling public to identify with it. The name and symbol in close association were used on the fascias of offices, on house specification sheets and on all company stationery. The design itself was naturally taken through to 'For Sale' garden boards, which are essential elements in an estate agent's projection. In order to maintain the developing stance of a very modern, up-to-date company, the traditional garden board, usually made of plywood, hardboard, etc. was rejected and the company, in conjunction with the agency, pioneered the use of a garden board engineered in metal. This development was negotiated through an engineering company specializing in the production of motorway and other road signs. It proved to be a significant development and reflected clearly the forward-looking attitude and style being developed for the new company.

Having resolved the need to find a clear and simple logo in support of the Whitegates name, it became necessary to find a copy statement to be used in association with this logo which would, ideally, encapsulate the basic company philosophy. As a result, the supporting copy statement was developed as 'Tomorrow's kind of estate agent'. This copy claim was again a deliberate attempt to set the new organization apart, in an aggressive and modern way, from the traditional, locally entrenched estate agents. If the marketing and advertising stance was going to be effective then it was felt that a lot of new ground had to be broken in order to establish 'Tomorrow's kind of estate agent'. (By tradition, the field of estate agency is one that attracts little consumer interest and awareness – even the biggest organizations in the market tend to be old-fashioned and appear to have time-worn attitudes towards advertising and promotion. They are incredibly bad at projecting a forward-looking and efficient image.)

Consideration was given to a variety of creative strategies to support the need to project a modern, forward-looking company, and a number of approaches were developed to review stage including the use of various personalities. The idea of using a personality to give credibility and authority to the new service gained ground as the creative work was being developed and a number of candidates were considered.

At this time, when the whole basic creative strategy was being developed, Raymond Baxter had just finished a prolonged period as the presenter of the then highly successful 'Tomorrow's World' programme. The agency decided that he was just the right personality to give aggression, authority, credibility and style to the new company. After detailed negotiations, a series of television commercials was developed using Raymond Baxter (who agreed to undertake the role partly because of the forward-thinking attitude the company represented). Full use was made of Raymond Baxter's presentation style in a dramatic 'limbo' format to add weight to the fact that Whitegates was 'Tomorrow's kind of estate agent'.

The initial series of television advertisements, consisting of two 30-second commercials and four 15-second commercials, all used Raymond Baxter's personality and style to full effect. The 30-second commercials were structured to sell the fullest aspects of the service, one appealing to buyers and one appealing to sellers, with 15-second support commercials being used to accentuate each of the main points in the selling platform, e.g. the efficient computer controlled system, fixed fees, opening hours, the *Property Weekly*, etc. The plan was to use television for an eight-week continuous and heavy burst of activity to establish the Whitegates name and service, making specific reference to the branch offices in both Leeds and Bradford.

As the operation expanded and more branches were opened, so the local Yorkshire TV rate was no longer available to the company. But because of the earlier success and response it was decided to continue to use television at regional rates, supported by a relatively low level of press advertising in selected evening and weekly newspapers. Three follow-up bursts of TV activity took place following the initial eight-week launch campaign: March (four weeks), May/June (nine weeks) and September/October (eight weeks) - all using the same combination of 30-second and 15-second commercials.

MEASURING THE SUCCESS OF THE CAMPAIGN

It will by now be clear that 'hard' measurement criteria such as sales are difficult to apply in this case history. However, the criteria which can be used, and which are most relevant, are the factors of growth and expansion of the new company, measurement of consumer attitudes, awareness and behavioural evidence, and, most significantly, the company's position in the market place (starting from a position of non-existence).

Let's look first at growth and expansion.

Within the first year of trading (1978), Whitegates Estate Agency developed from having just two branches in Leeds and Bradford to having well established and successful offices in eight locations, including the prime centres of Sheffield, Hull and Barnsley.

Eight offices within twelve months - six of which were not even planned at the time the new company was launched in Bradford and Leeds in January 1978.

Because of the level of success and proven reaction to the 1978 television campaign, heavy use of the television medium continued throughout 1979. A new series of television commercials was produced, still featuring Raymond Baxter but now using an even more aggressive and confident style. By this time, more extensive use of local press had also been introduced to support the television activity. Each new branch opening, because of the 'softening' of the ground by the television campaigns, produced an ever-increasing stock of properties, to the extent that, in some cases, the initial stock almost became an embarrassment to the company.

Continued expansion through new branch openings took place in 1979, leading to the position in May 1980 where the company had twenty branches operating. This rapid build-up meant that Whitegates was established in almost all of the major population centres originally identified as the prime targets. Centres not yet represented were largely for reasons of lack of planning permission and/or failure to obtain satisfactory branch locations.

By the end of 1979 (two years after the launch), Whitegates Estate Agency was by far the biggest domestic estate agency in Yorkshire. In market share terms, *the company now (May 1980) holds at least 15 per cent of the total Yorkshire market*, has a stock of properties well in excess of 2000 spanning all types and values of property, and would claim to be the biggest domestic estate agency in the North of England - an incredible performance!

MEASURED BY RESEARCH

The part that effective advertising has had to play in this success story is perhaps best illustrated by an independent image study which was conducted by Scantel Research Limited for Whitegates *only eleven months* after the company commenced to trade.

This research consisted of two stages, using both qualitative and quantitative techniques. The results of the qualitative stage were used as an input into the quantitative stage, and consisted of discussion between Scantel's consultant psychologists, the company's negotiators and an initial number of interviews with respondents known to be selling their homes. The quantitative stage was in two parts, one designed for Whitegates users and one for non-users with interviews carried out in both the Leeds and Bradford areas.

The *unprompted awareness* of Whitegates *was higher than for any competing estate agency* and the *prompted awareness of Whitegates was 100 per cent* – this, in spite of the relatively recent appearance of the company on the market. Almost 85 per cent of Whitegates users mentioned television or press advertisements as their main source of awareness of the company. It must be remembered that many of the company's competitors have been trading in the areas concerned for as many as 50 years and yet *only one* other company achieved an unprompted awareness level comparable to Whitegates.

The following extracts from the Summary, Conclusion and Recommendations of the Research Report are relevant:

(*Scantel Research*, *Project No. 569, November 1978*)

5.0 SUMMARY AND CONCLUSIONS

'Non-users exhibited *a high level of unprompted awareness of Whitegates* and awareness was *100 per cent under prompted* conditions.

'A significant proportion of non-users claimed that they would have used Whitegates had they known about the company at the time of selecting an agent [the decision having been made to sell, and an estate agent appointed, prior to the Whitegates launch].

'Around 85 per cent of users had come to *know about Whitegates* through either television commercials or press advertisements.

'In contrast, most users of competitors had acquired their knowledge through personal experiences and/or contact.'

6.0 RECOMMENDATIONS

'Television and press campaigns have been extremely powerful in attracting customers to Whitegates. *Indeed on the evidence of this research, the launch campaign has been fundamental to the success of Whitegates, and we have no reason for believing that continued growth could be achieved without heavy and continuous promotional support.*'

The latest research findings re-confirm the part that television advertising has had to play in the Whitegates success. This research, undertaken by the Marketing Division of Provident Financial Group during September 1980, was to examine clients' attitudes immediately after the appointment of Whitegates to handle the sale of their property.

The research was conducted by post among 1000 customers, 42 per cent of whom responded to the survey. The resulting sample (used for analysis) was well stratified in terms of age/social grade of respondents, value of property, and location within Yorkshire.

Within this research questionnaire, clients were asked the source of their knowledge of Whitegates, viz: 'How did you first hear about Whitegates before you approached them?' Provision was made for more than one source to be indicated.

The result of this section of the survey is quoted from the report:

'TV emerges as the most powerful medium of information, being mentioned almost as often as all the other sources combined. TV is weaker in Harrogate and York where viewing is partially split between Yorkshire TV and Tyne Tees TV.

'The three main sources are analysed below:

	Solus mention		Mentioned with other		Total	
	No.	%	No.	%	No.	%
TV	161	38.2	131	31.1	292	69.3
Press	39	9.3	98	23.3	137	32.5
Recommendation	44	10.5	65	15.4	109	25.9

'With nearly 4 out of 10 respondents mentioning TV as the sole source, the strategy of spearheading promotional activity with this medium is confirmed. Detailed analysis of those giving TV a solus mention shows that proportionally rather more under-35s (about 5 per cent) gave this source than the two older age groups. However there was no discernible difference in the levels of TV mention in cases where the respondents were using an estate agent for the first or subsequent times, nor did the value of the property influence the levels.

'Press advertising alone would be unlikely to maintain adequate awareness but has its part to play more probably for the person who is already in a buying or selling situation. It has a rather stronger appeal to the older age groups.'

At a level of 69.4 per cent, TV advertising emerges as the most powerful medium of information – the strongest possible statement of advertising effectiveness!

CONCLUSIONS

Despite involvement in many previous marketing successes over a period of years, the agency has never been associated with an advertising campaign the effectiveness of which can be so clearly demonstrated as has been the case with the launch of Whitegates Estate Agency.

Not only is the company now extremely well established in its territory, having expanded at a rate far in excess of any of the forecasts made, but it has also broken new ground in promoting services which have hitherto not been effectively advertised through the television medium.

Indeed, such is the level of success that Trident Television now consider the Whitegates growth story so highly that they have used it for the promotion of their own television stations, through mailings, press releases and articles.

Of the 22 target centres in the Yorkshire Television region originally planned for the development programme, the company now has representation in almost all of them; and those which are not yet covered are at advanced stages in the future expansion plans.

Whilst the backbone of the advertising effort was effective television, this was supported by many other marketing elements, i.e. press advertising, sales brochures and shop fascias, all clearly showing the creative stance of Whitegates – 'Tomorrow's kind of estate agent'.

We submit that this campaign represents a proven and convincing case for the effectiveness of advertising.

There can be few products or services which have developed to market leadership in an established and highly competitive market in less than two and a half years. Whitegates Estate Agency and ourselves are convinced that this could not have been achieved without the help of the effective advertising campaign and strategy developed for them: a campaign of which our clients and we are justly proud.

4

The Effect of Television Advertising on the Launch of Deep Clean

INTRODUCTION

This paper describes the launch of a new denture cleaning brand, Deep Clean, and the methods used to evaluate the effects of advertising on its initial sales. Generally, it is very difficult to distinguish the influence of advertising from all the other forms of promotional activity that attend the launch of a brand, e.g. money-off coupons, in-store promotional display and the simple fact that the brand is in distribution and therefore available. However, the advertising support for Deep Clean took the form of a national press campaign in newspapers and consumer magazines with an additional substantial weight of television advertising in two areas, Lancashire and Yorkshire. It is the latter feature which is important because it provided the opportunity to isolate the effect of television advertising on sales.

The analysis showed that the additional television activity doubled the brand's market share. This outcome is regarded as a commercial success, since the additional expenditure involved should be repaid within two years.

BACKGROUND TO THE LAUNCH OF DEEP CLEAN

Market Background

In 1978 Steradent (a Reckitt & Colman product) was the brand leader in the large, but declining, specialist denture cleaner market. However, whilst Steradent was the dominant brand, it was also potentially vulnerable, particularly in the grocery trade. There were three or four major manufacturers with both the expertise and resources to challenge Steradent's position in the UK. Efferdent, for example, launched by Warner Lambert in 1970, achieved a 17 per cent brand share during its first year. It was against this background that Reckitt & Colman began to examine ways of securing the specialist denture cleaning market in the UK.

Steradent is an alkaline cleaner which, if used regularly, removes film and plaque from dentures and prevents the build-up of stain carrying deposits on dentures. However, because Steradent is formulated principally to be effective against plaque and film, its efficacy in removing calculus (commonly known as tartar) is limited.

Deep Clean was developed to overcome this problem. An acid denture cleaner in tablet form, it was the first of its kind in the world.

Positioning

The obvious positioning for Deep Clean was as a superior denture cleaner dealing with a particular problem suffered by a segment of the denture wearing population. However, some interesting results emerged from a product placement test carried out in November 1978. Before trial, respondents were shown the pack with a simple product concept statement. Although speed of cleaning was only mentioned in the body copy, this was picked out as the major advantage rather than its superior cleaning effectiveness. This was a truly revealing commentary on the denture cleaning market. Steradent was seen as an overnight steeper taking a long time to work, and being without one's dentures for any long period of time is disliked by many denture wearers. Thus, a quick steeper, which was also effective, was seen by them as a major breakthrough.

The importance of speed as an incentive to trial was confirmed by advertising concept research carried out in April 1979. This showed Deep Clean to be viewed as a modern, fast acting and more effective denture cleaner than Steradent.

Media Strategy

It was decided that, for the launch of Deep Clean, national press advertising would be used, for the following reasons:

(a) The target audience for a specialist denture cleaner is old, defined loosely as all adults 35+, but more precisely four in five are over 45 and two in five are over 65.
(b) Despite the fact that older people tend to watch more television than younger age groups, experience across a wide range of products demonstrates a consistently lower level of advertising recall by older age groups. We would hypothesize that part of the reason for this may be due to the very rapid nature of TV communication. With press, on the other hand, once interested, a denture wearer could take things at his/her own pace.

It was felt, however, that a combination of both press and television advertising could provide a powerful impetus to the product's sales, especially amongst denture wearers under 50 years old, and thus the decision was taken to advertise on television in two regions, Yorkshire and Lancashire. Yorkshire was chosen as a test area on the basis of its average characteristics in terms of denture-wearing population and usership of specialist denture cleaners. A higher level of television advertising support was employed in Lancashire, to counter the test market launch of 'Extradent', a new product from a competitive manufacturer.

Creative Execution

Advertising concept research was conducted in April 1979. On the basis of the findings, a launch press advertisement was developed which emphasized speed and featured a fizzing tablet which communicated speed, activity and freshness. The visual mnemonic was in-

'Clean as a Whistle'

SUNG There's a great denture cleaner that in ten minutes flat

Can get your dentures so fresh and so clean

As clean as a (*whistle*)

in ten minutes they'll be

As clean as a (*whistle*) You'll see!

MVO With Deep Clean stains and bacterial plaque disappear to leave your dentures fresh and clean in just ten minutes

SUNG Oh as clean as a (*whistle*) you'll see what we mean

with super fresh Deep Clean

MVO Deep Clean from Steradent . . . For dentures as clean as a (*big whistle effect*)

Stills from Deep Clean television advertisement.

New Steradent Deep Clean. The denture cleaner that only takes 10 minutes!

Try the 10 minute test

Pop your denture into a glass of warm water. Add one Deep Clean tablet. The low pH formula immediately releases the active cleaning ingredients in a fresh effervescent solution which breaks up and dissolves away tartar deposits and stains.

10 minutes later rinse and look – your denture will definitely look cleaner. Really stubborn stains and heavy tartar deposits may need two or three treatments – but you will achieve a really clean denture in a very short time.

Finally try the tongue test (run your tongue over the denture). It doesn't just <u>look</u> much cleaner – it feels it too!

Deep Clean

Your denture has never been so clean – so fast!

Deep Clean press advertisement.

cluded in the final TV execution which itself was based on a successful advertising concept, 'clean as a whistle'. It was felt that this would work better in a moving medium than it could in a static medium.

EVALUATION

Analysis of Sales Data

Deep Clean was launched in July 1979 and its sales performance, measured by Nielsen bi-monthly audits, is recorded in Figure 4.1. The graph shows the brand's share of all denture cleaner sales, together with the timing of the press and television advertising. There is clear evidence that, from the beginning of the television advertising, sales in both Lancashire and Yorkshire have increased at a far greater rate than in the rest of the country.

Whilst this is certainly a prima facie case for the effectiveness of television advertising, it is possible that other marketing factors were responsible for the improved sales in these areas. However, there is no evidence that this was the case. The average selling prices of Deep Clean and its competitors have not varied regionally; with the exception of Lancashire, which saw the introduction of Extradent, competitive activity and promotion has been uniform across the country; and consumer promotions for Deep Clean in the form of press coupons appeared nationally.

Another important factor is the availability of the brand, and Figure 4.2 records the growth of sterling-weighted shop distribution. This shows that levels of distribution were initially much the same in all areas, but latterly distribution in the televised areas, Lancashire and Yorkshire, exceeded that in the other areas by some ten points. This improvement could of course be the result of the television activity encouraging retailers to stock the brand. But even if this is not the case, the differences in distribution could not by themselves account for all of the sales improvement in Lancashire and Yorkshire. This is demonstrated in Figure 4.3 which plots the 'rate of sale' (i.e. market share per point of sterling shop distribution) achieved in each period.

Again, in comparison with the other areas, the rate of sale in Lancashire and Yorkshire improved dramatically from the commencement of the television advertising. By January/February the rate of sale in Lancashire was double that of the other areas and in Yorkshire it was fifty per cent higher.

Cumulative Advertising Effects

Both the brand share and rate of sales results show that the brand's performance in Lancashire and Yorkshire was similar up until the January/February audit, at which point sales in Yorkshire fell back whilst sales in Lancashire continued to improve. This disparity can be explained by an examination of the achieved television rating in each area. In the latter months the weight of advertising in Yorkshire was substantially lower than that achieved in Lancashire. By the end of February the cumulative ratings in Yorkshire were 58 per cent of those in Lancashire (Yorkshire 803 TVR, Lancashire 1373 TVR).

To talk in terms of accumulated ratings since launch supposes that the advertising, once seen, is never forgotten. This is obviously fallacious since the effects of an advertising exposure are bound to diminish over time. This concept can be expressed by calculating the

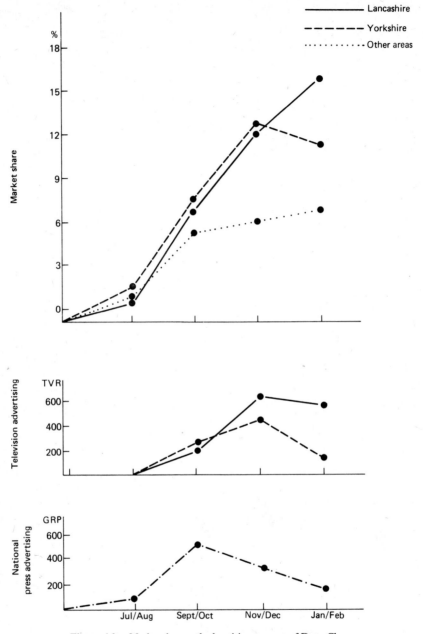

Figure 4.1.   Market share and advertising support of Deep Clean.

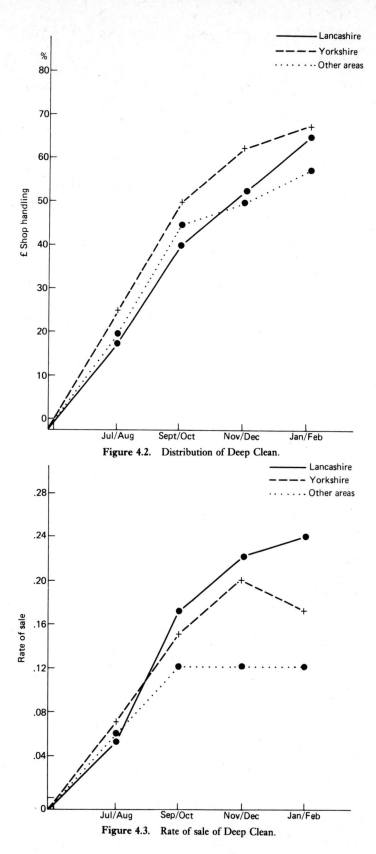

Figure 4.2. Distribution of Deep Clean.

Figure 4.3. Rate of sale of Deep Clean.

net accumulated weight of advertising, which is the sum of current advertising plus advertising seen in the past, the latter being discounted by an amount depending on the interval since it was first seen. Specifically, the calculation has the form:

Net accumulated advertising weight
$$= A_0 + \delta A_1 + \delta^2 A_2 + \ldots\ldots\ldots\ldots\ldots$$

where A_0 = Current advertising
$A_1 \ldots\ldots A_i$ = Advertising i periods ago
δ = the proportion of the advertising effect carried over to the next period.

The above concept was employed to model the incremental sales achieved by television advertising. A variety of values for the advertising decay rate were tried, the most satisfactory result being obtained by assuming the advertising effects decay at a rate of about 30 per cent per period. This is demonstrated in Figure 4.4, which shows how much of the actual sales variation is explained by alternative assumptions for the decay rate.

Figure 4.5 shows the incremental sales achieved in Lancashire and Yorkshire plotted against the net accumulated weight of advertising, expressed as effective TV ratings per

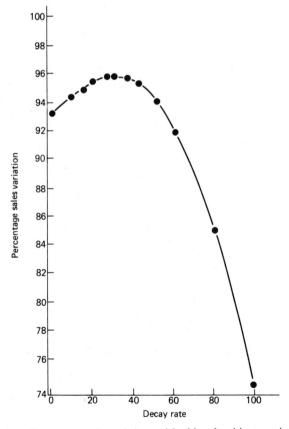

Figure 4.4. Percentage of sales variation explained by advertising at various decay rates.

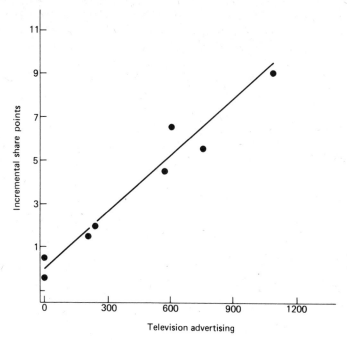

Figure 4.5. Correlation between incremental sales and TV advertising.

period. Whilst the estimate of the advertising decay rate is based on only a limited number of data points, the hypothesis that the growth of sales during the launch period is dependent on the net accumulated weight of advertising does explain the difference in the brand's performance in the two areas.

Consumer Research

Further evidence for the effect of television advertising is available from an independent national survey of denture wearers carried out in March 1980, shortly after the end of the television campaign. The results are summarized in Table 4.1.

Both the awareness and brand last purchased scores in Lancashire and Yorkshire are roughly double the figures achieved in the rest of the country and this is consistent with the differences in market share shown by the Nielsen data.

TABLE 4.1: CONSUMER RESEARCH ON DEEP CLEAN, MARCH 1980

	Yorks/Lancs Base = 140	Rest of country Base = 337
Spontaneous brand awareness	8.5%	3.5%
Total brand awareness	31.0%	15.4%
% of people whose last purchase was Deep Clean	6.5%	3.0%

The differences in the awareness scores are statistically significant at the 95 per cent confidence level.

THE PROFITABILITY OF TELEVISION ADVERTISING

The sales attributable to television advertising can be calculated from the differences between the market share achieved in Lancashire and Yorkshire and the rest of the country. To date, the gross profit from these additional sales amounts to 26 per cent of the cost of the television advertising. However, this calculation understates the benefit from advertising for two reasons. Firstly, the residual effects of the advertising which has already appeared will induce further trial purchases, and, secondly, a proportion of those consumers who have already been motivated to make their first purchase will go on to become regular users of the brand. Thus the full benefits of the television advertising will be calculable only when the final levels of trial and repurchase are established. However, if the sales generated by TV advertising were to continue at their current level, then the cost of advertising would be repaid within a year.

Arguably such an assessment is optimistic, but evidence from the consumer survey carried out in March 1980 showed that, even nine months after the launch, a high proportion (58 per cent) of people buying Deep Clean were buying it for the first time, and that the average repurchase rate amongst those who were not first time buyers was 60 per cent. These figures would suggest that sales should continue at least half their current level, which would imply a pay-back period of under two years. Compared with the typical experience of new product launches, this is a highly satisfactory result and demonstrates the effectiveness of the advertising campaign.

Section Two

Established Products, Consumer Goods and Services

5

Dettol

A Case History

INTRODUCTION

In this case history we have set out to demonstrate in two distinct ways that Dettol's advertising works and is effective.

Firstly we show that, by virtue of a change in creative strategy that was implemented at the beginning of 1978, consumer attitudes to Dettol have been modified in the directions intended. The research also shows that the use and purchase of Dettol have increased in this period.

Secondly, an econometric analysis of factors affecting Dettol's sales during the period 1974–78 is used to demonstrate that the sales response to the advertising expenditures put behind Dettol generated profitable increases in sales.

Other factors influencing Dettol's sales are also identified and it is clear that two 'non-marketing' variables – seasonal factors and consumer's purchasing power (disposable income) – have a major effect.

We conclude however that it is the long term effects of Dettol advertising that lead consumers to purchase Dettol when these factors are favourable.

In consequence the dramatic decline in Dettol sales that occurred in 1975–77 was converted into an equally dramatic improvement in 1978 and maintained in 1979 (Table 5.1).

TABLE 5.1: DETTOL EX-FACTORY SALES INDEX

1973	100
1974	100
1975	85
1976	87
1977	83
1978	100
1979	100

Many brands enjoyed increased sales as a result of rising consumer prosperity in 1978, but not to the extent of these figures, which underline the importance of maintaining a brand franchise by sustained and effective advertising support.

BACKGROUND

Dettol has been marketed in the United Kingdom since 1933.

It is promoted as both an antiseptic and a disinfectant and is used in a wide variety of ways ranging from personal antisepsis of cuts and grazes, through to disinfection of surfaces in the kitchen and bathroom and, in some instances, as a more general disinfectant down lavatory bowls, waste pipes and drains. It is sold in three sizes, 100, 250 and 500 ml.

Dettol is not only a mature brand but an extremely well established one. There is universal awareness of it by housewives; 70 per cent of housewives claim to use it nowadays – a figure which has not changed over the past eight years; and it has virtually 100 per cent distribution in chemists and grocers.

Although there are many alternative antiseptics and disinfectants on the market, including many low priced retailer own brands, there is only one other product that is promoted as a direct alternative to Dettol in its range of uses, Savlon Liquid. For many years Savlon had been available only through chemist shops, but since the beginning of 1979 has been heavily advertised and its distribution widened into grocery outlets also.

Advertising support for Dettol has been provided consistently over the last 20 years and is considered to have been a major factor in the brand's development to the position it now occupies as described above. The case history described in the following pages, however, relates to the period 1974–1979 and describes, in particular, the changes to the advertising campaign that were implemented in 1978.

The 1977 Scenario

Sales of Dettol had reached a peak in 1973–74. However, a combination of factors – rapid inflation and declining consumer purchasing power, reduced advertising investment, some production problems – had led to a sharp decline in sales in 1975, 1976 and 1977 (see Table 5.1).

Additionally, a situation had been developing which was of concern to the future promotion of Dettol. A significant personal use of Dettol was in bathing which involved claims which could not be proved or disproved. Therefore, the ITCA would not permit the claims for this area of usage to be advertised.

So the problem that Reckitt & Colman and the agency faced in 1977 can be concisely expressed as: 'How can we restore sales volumes to the 1973–74 levels when a major usage area of Dettol is no longer open to direct advertising, and inflationary pressures are affecting sales volumes?'

DEVELOPMENT OF THE 1978 STRATEGY

Where is Increased Volume Going to be Obtained?

Research had shown that amongst Dettol users its use as an antiseptic was virtually universal; fewer housewives used it in its disinfectant role. Further research using diary panel techniques showed that there were certain household cleaning functions where Dettol was more widely used than others, e.g. in wiping lavatory seats, cleaning up after pets, but even in these instances Dettol's share of products used was relatively low.

We nevertheless argued that, to increase Dettol volume sales to any marked extent:

(i) We could not expect to obtain additional users – household penetration was extremely high (70 per cent).
(ii) And that increased volume was more likely to occur from the advertising of *disinfectant* uses of the product.

But this conclusion presented its own problems:

(i) The earlier success of Dettol had been built on the personal/antiseptic uses of the product: heavy promotion of disinfectant uses could well destroy the extremely favourable attitudes housewives had with regard to its personal benefits.
(ii) Dettol's price was considered to be a problem in the market place (dictated by the high cost of ingredients). If Dettol is looked upon primarily as a disinfectant then the price differential with its main alternatives become particularly large – in some instances two or three times the price of own label disinfectants.

How Should We Approach the Problem of Price?

An econometric analysis (described in full later) had shown that consumers appeared to be relatively insensitive to changes in Dettol's *price*, but sales were found to be affected by the decline in *disposable income*. This apparent anomaly can be explained by the fact that the housewife's need for Dettol has a lower priority than essential items such as food. In other words, for Dettol to be included in a housewife's grocery purchases, she must have sufficient money left after buying the essential items; and relatively small variations in the price of Dettol do not therefore affect her decision to buy. As a result the decision was taken to allow the price to rise generally in line with inflation and to confine any price cutting to short term, tactical retail promotions.

A New Creative Strategy Based on Disinfectant Usage

In developing a creative strategy for Dettol based on disinfectant usage it was essential to be aware of consumer perceptions of Dettol and to provide advertising consonant with them. Research had shown that advertising centred on the *scientific* basis for Dettol's performance in killing bacteria was ineffective in changing consumer attitudes and behaviour. The high regard which consumers have for Dettol is based on confidence and trust derived from its history, its name, its smell and clouding in water. As one interviewee commented: 'You can't see germs being killed. I have to use Dettol to be sure.'

New advertising for Dettol had to reflect such attitudes.

1978 ADVERTISING

At the beginning of 1978 we introduced new TV and press advertising for Dettol which took account of the thinking outlined in the previous section.

TV: Two TV commercials, entitled 'Beginning' and 'Discovery'. These two commercials addressed themselves to the need for environmental protection in the home

Dettol Protects
Pure, safe Dettol keeps your lavatory a safe place for everyone,
day and night. Trust Dettol to protect your family's health.

in the context of a newborn baby and a toddler, Dettol providing protection and confidence. In parallel a TV commercial for Dettol Cream – an antiseptic cream – was also transmitted, assisting in the reinforcement of Dettol's traditional first aid usage.

Press: Full colour page advertisements were produced in both 1978 and 1979 pinpointing specific disinfectant usage areas for Dettol. The subjects chosen were ones in which Dettol already had relatively high usage, although still low in absolute terms, viz: the lavatory seat, kitchen waste bins, cleaning where pets have been, e.g. the kitchen floor.

Media: In each of 1978 and 1979, TV advertising amounted to approximately 20 weeks at an average of 50 to 60 TVR per week in all ITV regions. The press advertisements appeared in women's weekly and monthly magazines providing 70 per cent cover and 7.0 OTS.

To summarize the advertising changes:

CONTENT

A switch from advertising which had been primarily concerned with the antiseptic uses of Dettol to its environmental/disinfectant role.

WEIGHT

Although the budget was maintained in cash terms in 1978, due to media cost inflation the effective weight of advertising was reduced by about 20 per cent compared to 1977.

RESULTS AND EVALUATION

1. Volume sales of Dettol increased substantially in 1978, and this achievement was maintained in 1979 (see Table 5.1).
2. Consumer research clearly indicates the improvements in consumer attitudes to Dettol that occurred during the period of the 1978–79 advertising campaign as well as changes in consumer usage of Dettol.
3. An econometric analysis of the factors affecting Dettol sales volume conducted over the period 1974–78 shows the profitability of the advertising investment throughout that period and suggests also that the long term investment in advertising is a major factor in determining consumer purchasing of Dettol.

It should be noted that the periods covered by the econometric analysis and the consumer research are not exactly coincident. The reason for this is simply that the two pieces of research were not planned as a co-ordinated programme.

Consumer Research

Two disinfectant and antiseptic usage and attitude studies have been carried out amongst consumers: the first in January 1978, the second in January 1980. These two surveys reflect the extent to which the advertising for Dettol has been successful, both in increasing its usage and changing perceptions of the brand.

The broad objectives of these studies were to monitor trends in the usage and image of disinfectants and antiseptics in terms of the following:

(i) Brand awareness
(ii) Brand penetration
(iii) User profiles
(iv) Usage patterns for the major brands
(v) The image of the major brands
(vi) Detailed purchasing habits
(vii) Usage and purchase patterns of antiseptic creams
(viii) Advertising recall

THE RESEARCH METHOD

For each of the studies, 1200 housewives were interviewed at 120 sampling points throughout Great Britain by Public Attitude Surveys Ltd. They were located by means of Random Location Sampling. In each case the sample was restricted to housewives aged 15 to 64.

A non-interlocking, two-way quota was set on working status (working full time/others) and whether they had children.

Weighting factors were applied to ensure that the sample was representative of the population.

THE FINDINGS

In the two year period since the beginning of the new Dettol strategy, research indicates that Dettol has:

(i) Retained its leading position in terms of the penetration measurements.
(ii) Achieved increases in terms of the frequency with which it is bought and used.
(iii) Achieved increases in the applications for which it is used, reflecting the success of the advertising strategy of the past two years.
(iv) Achieved positive shifts in its image as a disinfectant.
(v) Retained its positive image as an antiseptic.

There has been a substantial and significant increase in the frequency with which Dettol is used (Table 5.2). Just over one quarter (an increase of 7 percentage points) of users now use Dettol every day. 53 per cent of housewives use it on average every two to four days.

There has been a substantial and significant increase, of 10 percentage points, in the number of housewives buying Dettol once a month or more often (Table 5.3). These findings are consistent with the increase in ex-factory dispatches during 1978 and 1979 and the improvement in consumer sales audited by Nielsen, which is described overleaf.

In terms of usage, Table 5.4 shows increases in the areas of Dettol usage which clearly reflect the positive effects of the advertising strategy over the past two years. This table also shows that increased household usage has not resulted in a decline in personal usage – in fact, upward movements have been noted in some areas of personal use.

TABLE 5.2: THE FREQUENCY OF USING DETTOL

Base: all current users	January 1978 835 %	January 1980 849 %	Change 1980 vs. 1978
Every day	19	26	+7[a]
Every 2–3 days	28	27	−1
Every 4–6 days	12	11	−1
Once a week	19	18	−1
Once every 2–3 weeks	6	6	—
Once a month	7	5	−2
Less often	8	7	−1

[a] Statistically significant at 99.9 per cent confidence level.

TABLE 5.3: THE FREQUENCY OF BUYING DETTOL

Base: all current users	January 1978 835 %	January 1980 849 %	Change 1980 vs. 1978
Once a month or more often	39	49	+10[a]
Once every 6 weeks	22	18	−4
2–3 times a year	29	26	−3
Once a year	7	5	−2
Less often	3	2	−1

[a] Statistically significant at 99.9 per cent confidence level.

TABLE 5.4: THE USAGE OCCASIONS FOR DETTOL

Base: all current users	January 1978 835 %	January 1980 849 %	Change 1980 vs. 1978
Selected Household Uses			
Cleaning lavatory seat	51	56	+5[a]
Lavatory bowl	43	46	+3
Bath and handbasin	32	36	+4
Kitchen rubbish bins	29	34	+5[a]
Kitchen sink and waste pipe	28	32	+4
Kitchen floor	23	32	+9[c]
After pets	23	25	+2
Kitchen surfaces	16	23	+7[c]
Outside dustbin	13	14	+1
Selected Personal Uses			
Cuts and grazes	64	71	+7[b]
Bath	55	55	—
Bites and stings	38	45	+7[b]

Statistically significant at:
[a] 95 per cent confidence level.
[b] 99 per cent confidence level.
[c] 99.9 per cent confidence level.

The image questions were structured so that respondents could make a free association with attitude couplets by brand. Thus, the respondents were introduced, by a preamble, to mention whatever brands on the list were appropriate to the Stimulus (attitude couplets). The respondents were free to mention as many or as few brands as they wished. In each study half the sample were given a list of antiseptic brands to associate with the attitude couplets while the other half of the sample were given a list of disinfectant brands.

Table 5.5 shows the number of positive mentions achieved by Dettol over several selected dimensions. Aside from illustrating the positive overall image of Dettol, it also shows upward shifts in perceptions of the brand's image in those areas for which it has been advertised.

Table 5.6 shows the number of positive mentions achieved by Dettol when the product is rated amongst a list of other antiseptics, and illustrates the overall stability of the brand in this area.

TABLE 5.5: THE IMAGE OF DETTOL AS A DISINFECTANT

Base: all rating the disinfectant products	January 1978 583 %	January 1980 592 %	Change 1980 vs. 1978
A product you can really trust	91	94	+3[a]
Particularly effective against infection	90	90	—
Strong enough for my needs	83	82	−1
Goes a long way	73	73	—
Particularly suitable for cleaning the lavatory	52	56	+4
Particularly suitable for sinks and drains	47	50	+3
Particularly suitable for kitchen surfaces	37	41	+4

[a] Statistically significant at 95 per cent confidence level.

TABLE 5.6: THE IMAGE OF DETTOL AS AN ANTISEPTIC

Base: all respondents rating the antiseptic products	January 1978 614 %	January 1980 602 %	Change 1980 vs. 1978
A product you can really trust	92	92	—
Particularly effective against infection	88	86	−2
Strong enough for my needs	82	82	—
Particularly suitable for adding to bath water	78	77	−1
Goes a long way	66	66	—

Econometric Analysis of the Factors Affecting Dettol Sales

OUTLINE OF METHOD OF ANALYSIS

Common sense dictates that variations in the weight or content of the advertising are not the only factors which will influence a brand's sales. Even with the benefit of a carefully controlled area test specifically designed to measure the effects of advertising, it is usually necessary to check and allow for the influence of other marketing factors which may have caused a differential sales effect between areas. In the case of Dettol, no controlled experiment was carried out and thus the evaluation of the sales effects of Dettol's advertising requires that any other influences on sales are isolated.

In essence, the method involves setting up a simple hypothetical model of the market which describes the likely relationship between the brand's sales and the marketing factors which are believed to influence sales. For example, a very simple model might be of the form:

$$\text{Brand Sales} = K_1 . \text{ Advertising} - K_2 . \text{ Price} + \text{Constant}.$$

This means that for each unit increase in advertising weight the brand's sales increase by K_1 units; and for each unit price increase sales will decrease by K_2 units. The technique of multilinear regression analysis is then used to find the values of the constants in the model (the K's) which provide the best fit to the historical sales data.

There are, of course, many different formulations of the model which are hypothetically possible, which then raises the question as to which is the right one. To answer this, the chosen model must satisfy three basic criteria:

(i) The model must agree with common sense. In other words, the variables influencing sales must satisfy our intuitive understanding of the market.

(ii) The model must be capable of accounting for a large proportion of the historic sales variation. Unless this is so, one cannot tell whether the marketing variables in the model really do significantly affect sales.

(iii) The model must be able to predict future sales once the new values of the various marketing variables are known. This last condition is an acid test of whether the model really does explain the behaviour of the market.

The mechanics of the analysis involve the use of real-time computer facilities. With this aid it is possible to evaluate many different models rapidly and at low cost, and thereby find a model which meets the three conditions described above. The following sections describe the evaluation of Dettol's sales performance. Details of the statistical analysis are shown in the appendix at the end of this chapter.

THE CONSTRUCTION OF THE MODEL

Dettol occupies a unique position in that it is used both as a disinfectant and an antiseptic; consequently the definition of its competitors, and hence its market share, is somewhat arbitrary. In the event, we found that the most satisfactory explanation of the brand's sales performance was achieved by modelling Dettol's actual volume sales rather than its share of a defined market.

The model was constructed from Nielsen bimonthly consumer sales audit data covering the period 1974–77, and the 1978 data were then used to test the model's predictive capability. (In the initial stages national data were used, which provided 30 observations, and the analysis was subsequently expanded by including the data for five individual regions, giving a total of 150 observations.)

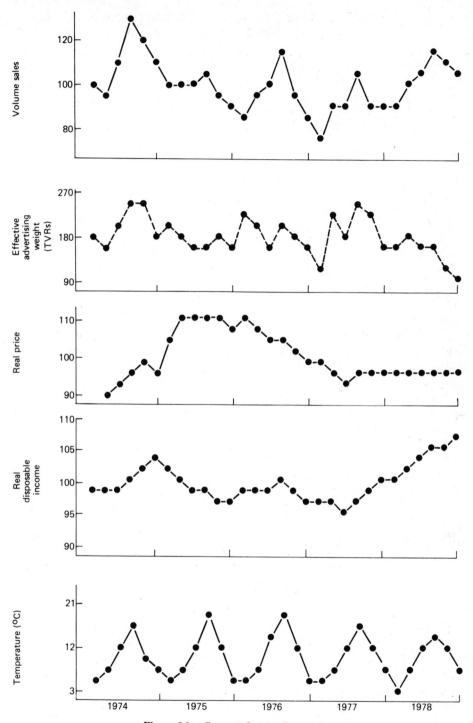

Figure 5.1. *Factors influencing Dettol sales.*

Four factors were found to have a statistically significant influence on Dettol sales; they were:

(i) Real personal disposable income.
(ii) Dettol's price (adjusted by the retail price index).
(iii) An underlying seasonal variation (this is common to all disinfectants and antiseptics, sales being higher in the warmer summer months).
(iv) Accumulated advertising weight (described in detail in the next section).

Figure 5.1 shows how each of these factors has varied over time. When combined they account for 90 per cent of all the variations in Dettol's national sales. This is demonstrated in Figure 5.2, which shows the bimonthly sales of Dettol as recorded by Nielsen from 1974 to 1977, together with the fit to these data provided by the model which has the four factors above as its components. In statistical terms the correlation between sales and the component factors is highly satisfactory; the chance that the result is merely a random coincidence is substantially less than one in a thousand.

The significance of the relationship between sales and each individual factor is demonstrated by the cross-plots shown in Figures 5.3 to 5.6. For example, Figure 5.3 shows the correlation between the variation in accumulated advertising weight (expressed as an effective advertising weight in TVRs) and Dettol sales after removing the effect of the other three factors (price, disposable income and seasonal variation).

An important feature of the analysis is the substantial effect that the 'non-marketing' variables have on sales. Together, the underlying seasonal variations and the influence of disposable income account for more than half of the total variation in Dettol's sales. This underlines the need to take account of such effects before examining the influence of factors which are within the control of the advertiser, i.e. price and advertising.

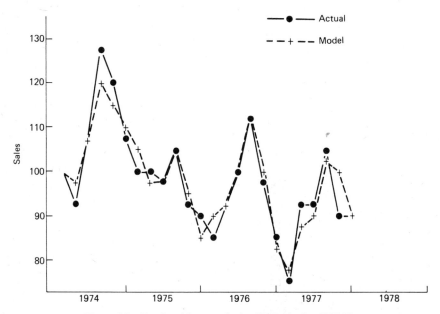

Figure 5.2   *Fit of model to actual sales. National sales, 1974–77.*

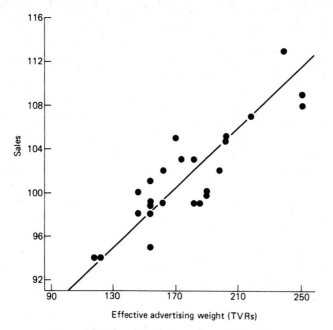

Figure 5.3. *Correlation between sales and advertising.*

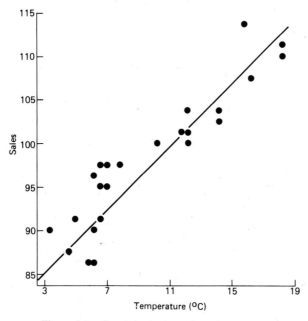

Figure 5.4. *Correlation between sales and temperature.*

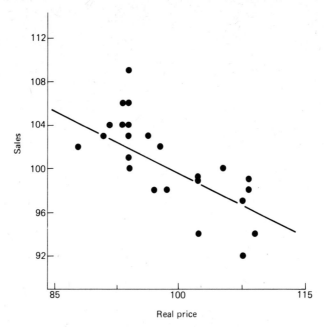

Figure 5.5.   *Correlation between sales and price.*

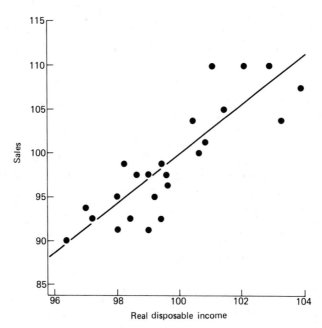

Figure 5.6.   *Correlation between sales and disposable income.*

The predictive capability of the model was tested by comparing the model's sales forecasts (based on the known values of the four variables during 1978) with the actual sales achieved in that period. This is shown in Figure 5.7. The model estimates closely follow the actual sales achieved, which is a very satisfactory result, particularly in view of the fact that the reversal of the previously declining sales trend has been correctly predicted.

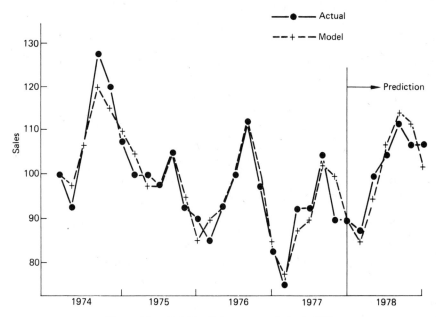

Figure 5.7. *Model predictions vs. actual sales in 1978.*

THE EFFECTS OF ADVERTISING

The weight of advertising was expressed in terms of television rating points. Press expenditure, which formed only a small proportion of the total, was included in the television figures assuming it to be equally cost efficient. Using the larger sample of 150 observations available from the regional Nielsen data, it was possible to investigate the duration of the advertising effect, i.e. previous advertising influencing sales in the current period. The analysis (which is described in the appendix) provided strong evidence that the advertising effect decayed over time at a rate of about 10 to 15 per cent per month, i.e. half the full sales effect is achieved within about four months. This is an important result since it means that it is the accumulated weight of advertising which influences sales and not simply the advertising in the current period.

THE ECONOMIC IMPLICATIONS

One of the most important features of this type of statistical analysis is that it is possible to quantify the effects on sales of changing the price and the weight of advertising. Because Nielsen reports at bimonthly intervals, and hence the number of observations is limited, only the average effect over a number of years can be calculated with any degree of reliability.

The results shown in Table 5.7 are presented in the form of elasticities, i.e. the percentage change in sales that results from a 1 per cent change in each of the four variables.

The price and advertising effects are clearly of most interest to the advertiser, since they have a direct bearing on decisions regarding the marketing strategy. The most useful way of interpreting these results is to compare the estimated elasticities with the 'breakeven' values (Table 5.8).

TABLE 5.7: ELASTICITIES CALCULATED FROM ECONOMETRIC MODEL, 1974–78

	Best estimate	95% confidence range
Advertising elasticity	.19	.11–.26
Price elasticity	−.44	−.64−−.23
Disposable income elasticity	2.26	1.66–2.86
Temperature (pr^0C)	1.85	1.49–2.21

TABLE 5.8: ESTIMATED ELASTICITIES COMPARED WITH BREAKEVEN VALUES

	Best estimate	Breakeven
Advertising elasticity	.19	0.16
Price elasticity	−0.4	−2.0

For example, the breakeven price elasticity of −2.0 means that a 1 per cent increase in price would generate an increased profit for the brand provided that sales volume did not fall by more than 2 per cent. The estimate of the actual price elasticity is substantially less than this breakeven figure; had price been increased by 1 per cent the best estimate is that sales volume would have declined by 0.44 per cent. Thus, there is strong evidence that the brand has been underpriced.

By contrast, the estimate of Dettol's advertising elasticity, 0.19, is higher than the breakeven figure of 0.16 (this is the percentage increase in sales required to recover the costs of a 1 per cent increase in advertising expenditure).

The implications of this are:

(i) *The advertising expenditure over the period 1974–78 has generated profitable increases in sales for the brand.* Even allowing that a degree of uncertainty is associated with every statistical estimate, there is only a 1 in 5 chance that the advertising was not profitable (i.e. the advertising elasticity was actually less than breakeven).
(ii) Given that our best estimate of the advertising elasticity is correct, the level of expenditure should have been higher to maximize the profit returned. By definition, at the optimum expenditure level the breakeven and actual elasticities will be equal. However, it is not possible to say what the optimum level should have been; to do so requires that the precise shape of the advertising/sales relationship is known.

The consumer research described above showed that the 1978 advertising campaign had generated significant improvements in consumers' attitudes, accompanied by increases in claimed usage. This certainly suggests an increased advertising effectiveness in 1978. Unfortunately, it is not possible to confirm this finding via the econometric analysis, for two reasons:

1. Firstly, as previously stated, there are only a limited number of sales observations for any one year, which means that an estimate of the advertising elasticity based on one year's data will be very unreliable. In fact, a statistically significant result would only have been obtained had the advertising doubled in effectiveness.
2. Secondly, 1978 was a period when consumers' disposable income rose rapidly. In this situation it becomes very difficult to separate the contributions that advertising and disposable income made to the improvement in sales. (A very small change in the weight of importance given to disposable income would allow a substantial improvement in the effectiveness of the 1978 advertising.)

However, the assessment of the average advertising effectiveness over the period 1974–78 almost certainly understates the contribution that advertising made to the substantial improvement in sales during 1978. The rapid increase in consumers' spending power was a necessary precursor, but it is not axiomatic that this increased prosperity should have been directed to purchases of Dettol. Consumers must have a reason for purchasing the brand which involves a belief in its value, and this in large part must depend on the image built up by many years of advertising. Such benefits cannot be readily quantified, but they nevertheless provide additional justification to the value of Dettol's advertising.

CONCLUSION

The change in advertising strategy that occurred in 1978 provided us with the opportunity of demonstrating that Dettol's advertising does influence attitudes and behaviour. There were shifts in consumer usage and attitudes along each of the desired dimensions.

The econometric analysis conducted between 1974 and 1978 has shown that the advertising expenditure on Dettol in this period has been profitable.

Further, in 1978, the combination of past and current advertising allowed Dettol to capitalize on the growth in consumer spending power.

APPENDIX: TECHNICAL APPENDIX TO ECONOMETRIC ANALYSIS

1. Model Based on National Sales Data

The results shown below were achieved using stepwise multilinear regression on 24 observations, covering the period 1974–77.
The regression equation is:

Sales Volume = 1.7 × Temperature + 2.2 × Disposable Income
+ .183 × Accumulated Advertising − .241 × Real Price
− 131

With the exception of temperature (which is expressed in degrees centigrade) all other variables were computed as indices about their mean values and hence the coefficients represent the elasticities for each variable.
The key statistics for the regression equation are as follows:

$R^2 = .909$ This shows that 91 per cent of the variation in sales volume has been explained and thus it is unlikely that another factor of major importance has been ignored.

F ratio $= 35.85$ This means that the chance of such an explanation being due to random chance is less than one in a thousand.

Standard error as % of mean volume $= 4.13$
     This is a measure of the likely forecasting error.

Durbin-Watson statistic on residuals $= 1.8$
     It is important that the error term (residual variation) is randomly distributed. If this is not the case, then the variables are not independent of each other, and errors in estimation are likely. There is no evidence here of colinearity (a value of 2.0 is ideal, with 1.5 to 2.5 being acceptable limits).

The table below shows key statistics for each of the variables in the regression equation.

	$Mean^a$	95% Confidence limits		T $statistic^b$	$Partial$ F^c
		upper	lower		
Temperature	1.7	2.15	1.24	7.89	62.2
Disposable income	2.2	1.11	4.25	4.25	18.1
Advertising	0.18	0.07	3.47	3.47	12.1
Real price	-0.24	-0.52	-1.82	-1.82	3.3

[a] The mean is the most likely estimate of the coefficient for each variable, and the 95 per cent confidence limits indicate that there is a 5 per cent chance of the coefficients lying outside the range shown.
[b] The T statistic is a measure of the extent to which the coefficient is significantly different from zero (i.e. the variable has no effect on the regression equation). A value greater than 2.0 is significant at the 95 per cent confidence level.
[c] This is a test of whether the variable in question explains a significant amount of the sales variation. A value of 4.0 would be significant at the 95 per cent confidence level.

2. Model Based on Regional Data

The regional model was based on 150 observations using Nielsen data from the five largest areas (London, Midlands, Lancashire, Yorkshire, Wales and West). Each variable was expressed as its index about the regional mean.

The existence of long-term advertising effects was established by first testing for an immediate advertising effect and then by introducing lagged advertising variables, examining whether the fit of the model (R^2) improved significantly (an R^2 lower than that for the national model is to be expected, since the regional Nielsen shop sample is smaller). With only immediate advertising considered, the R^2 was .50 and the F ratio for immediate advertising 19.1; by including advertising variables successively lagged up to six periods ago, the R^2 improved to .58.

A plot of the lagged advertising coefficients is shown in Figure 5.8. Compared with the coefficient for immediate advertising, those for the lagged variables diminish the longer the lag. The rate of advertising decay implied by this is of the order of 25 per cent per bimonthly period.

This information was used to construct a transformed advertising variable, representing the accumulated advertising effect, assuming a decay rate of 25 per cent per bimonth, viz:

Accumulated Advertising Weight $= a_0 + .75a_1 + (.75)^2 a_2 + \ldots$
     where $a_0 =$ current advertising
     where $a_i =$ advertising lagged by i periods

Using this variable the R^2 achieved was .65, with the F ratio for advertising increasing to 57.5.
The full results were as follows:

Sales Volume = 1.85 × Temperature + 2.26 × Disposable Income
+ .188 × Accumulated Advertising − .44 × Real Price
$R^2 = .653$ F Ratio = 44.7
Standard error as % of mean volume = 8.3
Durbin-Watson statistic on residuals = 2.1

| | 95% Confidence limits | | T | Partial |
	upper	lower	statistic	F
Temperature	2.21	1.49	10.04	100.82
Disposable income	2.86	1.66	7.4	54.9
Advertising	0.264	0.111	4.86	23.6
Real price	−0.23	−0.64	−4.15	17.25

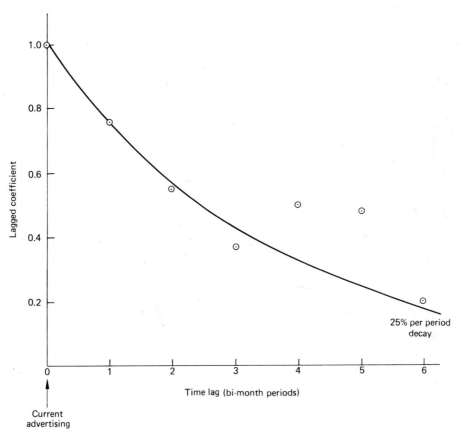

Figure 5.8. *Lagged advertising coefficients.*

6

Kellogg's Rice Krispies

The Effect of a New Creative Execution

BUSINESS BACKGROUND

Rice Krispies has been a major brand in the breakfast cereal market since it was first launched in the UK in 1929 – long enough to have been a part of most shoppers' own childhood. Its crisp puffs of toasted rice have a unique appeal to children: in a description made famous by advertising, they go 'Snap, Crackle, Pop' in milk.

The product itself is very light, so its average retail price per kilogram is about 50 per cent higher than market average, making it one of the more expensive brands. Sales volume has remained fairly constant around 10 million kilograms a year (Nielsen) for the last decade. Consequently, the brand's share of the growing cereal market declined slowly through most of the 1970s. Its share of ready-to-eat (RTE) cereal advertising declined more steeply, as its advertising levels in real terms were progressively reduced.

By 1977, volume share of market was down to 5.7 per cent according to Nielsen (though its sterling share of 8 per cent still made Rice Krispies the third largest brand by value). Rising costs of raw materials and the pressure on margins from the retail trade were making it increasingly difficult for the brand to fund the high advertising-to-sales ratio that historically it had needed to maintain consumer demand for this premium product. Furthermore, the falling birth-rate meant that its primary consumers – children – would be getting fewer.

So the advertising strategy was reviewed and a new creative execution was developed for 1978.

MARKETING AND ADVERTISING OBJECTIVES

The marketing aim was to win sales growth, in line with market growth at first in order to arrest the fall in share, and subsequently ahead of market in order to regain some, at least, of the share that had been lost. But with a shrinking child population – children eat over half the tonnage sold – this aim would be achieved only by increasing the numbers of families who buy Rice Krispies, and, in particular, by winning a share of their cereal purchases at the expense of other brands also largely eaten by children, such as Sugar Puffs and other pre-sweetened cereals, and Weetabix.

This meant, in fact, reversing the trend of previous years. Rice Krispies had been losing franchise because:

1. It was rather expensive, and needed to offer something extra to justify the cost of buying it regularly.
2. It was light and insubstantial, and so was thought to have little nourishment value in it, at a time when more mothers were setting store by substantiality and food value in their children's breakfast cereal.
3. Its image had become more of a hedonistic 'fun' cereal – suitable as an occasional treat for children – and less that of an everyday all-family staple.

The effect had been to make Rice Krispies seem to many of its consumers a less important brand than it really was. So they had demoted it from being one of their usual brands to being a secondary, occasional purchase.

Advertising was given the task of reversing these trends, of making Rice Krispies more important and more highly valued, and of putting it back into the role of an enjoyable staple breakfast food.

ADVERTISING STRATEGY

Central to the strategy we developed to meet these aims was the *uniqueness* of Rice Krispies, not just in its 'Snap, Crackle, Pop', but also in the power of this phrase to remind adults of when they too, as children, listened to Rice Krispies crackling and popping in a bowl of milk. More than any other cereal, it says childhood. It is *the* childhood cereal.

We wanted to evoke in parents their own memories of eating Rice Krispies when little, to remind them of the magic of the cereal that makes a noise – because, to its eaters, this magic has a very real value.

So we decided to present, in television commercials and in print advertisements, an appealing and credible portrayal of childhood. Firstly, to catch mothers' attention and interest, because what children *really* do and think always interests them. Secondly to evoke their own childhoods (so we would show only children, and no adults, in the advertisements, and try to present a world as seen through a child's eyes).

A third reason was that a truthful and sensitive representation of childhood would be evidence that Kellogg knew and cared about children and implicitly, therefore, about feeding them properly. (This was a high risk route, because the slightest dissonance or unreality caused by the child actors could, as many advertisements with children have done, easily trigger disbelief and dislike among the mothers watching, with wholly negative effect.)

Lastly, we wanted to remind people that whilst the magic of Rice Krispies is so much a part of childhood, the appeal of the brand is not child*ish*, but much wider than that; that it is not simply an occasional treat for the kids, but a sensible and worthwhile breakfast food that all the family can enjoy.

Out of this strategy developed a campaign that appeared to stand this last intention on its head. A series of television and magazine advertisements featured Edward, Rachel and the rest of their 'gang', and their attempts to start a national protest campaign to make adults *stop* eating Rice Krispies and to reserve it for children only: drafting speeches for the media, sending delegates to raise support in other towns, writing to the Prime Minister! (And thus, of course, calling attention to the fact that many adults do eat Rice Krispies!)

The new campaign began in the spring of 1978, using the same media mix of television and women's magazines as in previous years, and at no greater rate of real expenditure (Table 6.1). An industrial dispute at the plant in summer 1979 brought advertising to a halt for the rest of the year, but the campaign is now continuing in its third year in 1980.

TABLE 6.1: ADVERTISING LEVEL FOR RICE KRISPIES

		Annual television OTS[a] (Housewives)	Media expenditure at constant 1978 prices (MEAL) (£'000s)
	1976	17	1140
	1977	14	660
'Edward'	1978	13	600
campaign	1979 (Jan.–July)	9	350

[a] Average number of opportunities-to-see the television advertising per viewer per year.

EVALUATING THE EFFECT

Creative research during the development of the campaign suggested that the advertisements were achieving their aims. AGB's TCA audits of consumer purchasing revealed a sharp rise in the number of homes buying Rice Krispies each month, coinciding with the new campaign's start. Further analysis of buying patterns, from consumer panel data, showed that we were gaining in brand switching from Weetabix, instant porridge and the other competitive child cereals. Nielsen reported a $7\frac{1}{2}$ per cent sales volume growth in 1978, compared to a 3 per cent rise for the market in total. And apart from the period in 1979 when the brand was not available, sales have stayed buoyant.

The market indications are, then, that the campaign is on strategy and that it is working. More importantly, there is firm evidence that the new advertising increased the value that consumers put on the brand and thus raised demand for it, with a substantial and quantifiable effect on sales revenue.

Given the brand's price premium, relative price is naturally a major factor affecting demand. So much so, in fact, that the size of the price effect in month by month sales variations tends to swamp and obscure the effects of other variables. The logical step was to see if we could isolate, and remove, the price effect, and then look for an advertising effect. To do this, we examined TCA monthly data* for 1975–77 (the three years prior to the new 'Edward' campaign) for evidence of correlation between the relative price of Rice Krispies and demand for the brand.

The method we used was based on the economist's conventional 'demand curve', in which quantity purchased is related diagrammatically to price. In practice we have found it appropriate to take the *relative* quantity purchased (as represented by a brand's percentage share of market volume) and relate that to its *relative* price (expressed as a ratio of the average price in the market).

* Monthly audits, and the recording of actual prices paid, make TCA data more suitable than Nielsen for this technique. However, a cross-check using Nielsen data produced confirmatory findings.

Stills from Rice Krispies television advertisement: 'What's wrong Rachel?'

'Are you still worrying about the grown-ups eating our Rice Krispies?'

'Are you thinking that they'll never stop eating our snap, crackle and pop?'

'I know Rachel, but we have to keep on trying.'

'Come on Rachel, it'll be all right.'

During periods of market stability, the observed measures of brand share and relative price tend to conform to the conventional demand curve pattern when they are plotted on a graph. That is, a relative price rise will tend to reduce share of sales (demand), whereas a fall in the relative price will tend to be accompanied by a rise in brand share.

New marketing action, when it is successful, can be expected to produce points on the graph that do not conform to the previously observed demand curve. So the technique provides a powerful means of monitoring, over relatively short periods of time, the effect of changes in marketing actions.

In the Rice Krispies analysis, we looked at the relationship between the brand's share of all RTE volume sales and its relative price (indexed to the all-RTE price per kilogram). The results (Figure 6.1) showed a modest correlation between price and share of the three

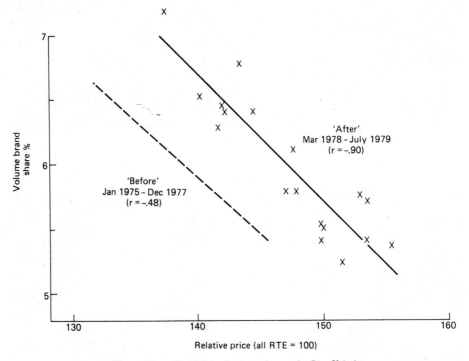

Figure 6.1.   *The shift in the demand curve for Rice Krispies.*

years 1975–77. Evidently other factors, in addition to price, were affecting demand. But the slope of the line* showed that Rice Krispies was fairly price sensitive, with a price elasticity of about −2. That is to say, a 5 per cent reduction in the price, from 140 on the price index scale to 133, could theoretically be expected to result in a rise in brand share from 5.9 to 6.5, a 10 per cent increase in sales volume. Or, to simplify, a 1 per cent fall in price would lead

---

* The economist's demand curve normally relates *proportionate changes* in sales to *proportionate changes* in price and is thus a straight line in the *logarithms* of the variables. But the increased accuracy of fitting such a curve across a fairly narrow range of price differences is not significant, and a straight line in natural values is a lot easier to use in practice.

to a 2 per cent rise in sales volume. However, it must be said again that the correlation ($-.48$) between relative price and sales for the period 1975–77 was not strong, and accounted for only one-quarter of observed sales variations.

From the start of the new campaign, however, the picture changed. The 1978–79 data showed a clear shift to the right in the demand line, and a closer correlation between price and market share.

It is worth noting that this was not a change in price sensitivity – the slope of the line is the same as before – but rather a rise in the perceived *value* of Rice Krispies accompanied by a rise in the proportion of month-by-month sales variation that was due to price.

This rise in brand value, which took place immediately after the start of the new 'Edward' campaign, continued at least until the market was disrupted in summer 1979. (It has taken time for the market to get back to normality since then. But first indications for Rice Krispies look good.) The difference between actual market shares achieved and those predicted by the previous years' price/share relationship was substantial, amounting to an additional 14 per cent in sales volume between March 1978 and July 1979, or an extra £$2\frac{1}{4}$ million in sales revenue (Figure 6.2).

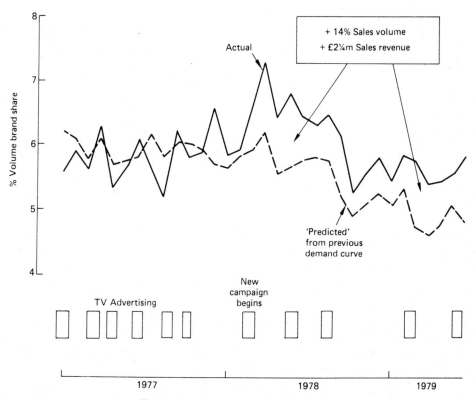

Figure 6.2. *The sales increase of Rice Krispies.*

How Much was the New Advertising Campaign Worth?

Something, it was clear, added value to the brand in the spring of 1978. The evidence that it was the change in advertising that was the cause is circumstantial, in that no other factor – neither distribution, sales force activity, on-pack promotion, nor competitors' action – could be judged to have changed anywhere near sufficiently to have brought about such a lasting shift in brand value. The only realistically plausible explanation which could be found was that the new advertising campaign did it.

Any creative stimulus that brings in over £2 million in extra sales in under 18 months is obviously valuable. But could a cash value, we wondered, be put on it? An approximate answer emerged from an analysis of the relationship between sales share and advertising share in the RTE cereal market.

To look at this, we used the 'Dynamic Difference' model,* which relates two factors:

1. The difference between this year's share of advertising (representing current marketing effort) and *last* year's brand share of market (representing the consumer franchise base before this year's advertising stimulus began).
2. The change in brand share between last year and this (representing the effect of the marketing effort).

The data are summarized in Table 6.2, and plotted graphically in Figure 6.3.

TABLE 6.2: MARKET AND ADVERTISING SHARES FOR RICE KRISPIES

	A Volume brand share	*B* Advertising expenditure share	*'Dynamic Difference' (B minus previous year's A)*	*Brand share change*
	%	%		
1970	7.0			
1971	7.4	14.3	+7.3	+0.4
1972	7.1	12.3	+4.9	−0.3
1973	7.0	11.2	+4.1	−0.1
1974	6.8	13.2	+6.2	−0.2
1975	6.2	10.2	+3.4	−0.6
1976	6.1	12.7	+6.5	−0.1
1977	5.7	8.5	+2.4	−0.4
1978	6.0	7.9	+2.2	+0.3

The results of this analysis showed a reasonably consistent relationship for 1971–77, followed by an exceptionally high market share achievement in 1978, when the brand gained 0.3 points. Such a gain, according to the regression equation for 1971–77, would have needed a Dynamic Difference of +8.5 points of advertising share in excess of brand share. In fact, the Dynamic Difference in 1978 was +2.2, so the effect of the campaign change was broadly comparable to the expected effect of an advertising expenditure increase of roughly 6.3 per cent of RTE cereals' advertising in 1978. According to MEAL, the market spent £7.6 million on advertising that year. So the extra sales effect on the new 'Edward' campaign was 'worth' the equivalent of about an additional £500 000 (6.3 per cent of £7.6m) spent on advertising in that year.

* Originated many years ago by M. J. Moroney of Unilever.

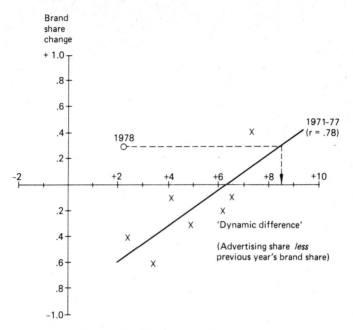

Figure 6.3.   *The Dynamic Difference model.*

The limitations of the data make this, at best, only a rough approximation. Nevertheless, they do suggest that the new strategy and execution just about doubled the effectiveness of the advertising.

CONCLUSIONS

We concluded that the new advertising had succeeded in its aims of making Rice Krispies a more important and more highly valued brand in consumers' eyes, and of rebuilding its role as a staple breakfast cereal.

On the basis of the evidence, we believe that:

1. The new campaign brought about a sustained increase in the value that consumers put on the brand.
2. This added value increased demand for the brand by about 14 per cent and brought in an additional £2¼ million in sales revenue inside 18 months.
3. This effect was very roughly equivalent to that of an extra £0.5 million a year spent on advertising.

THE METHOD OF EVALUATION

Growing experience of the 'demand curve' technique for assessing advertising's effects has convinced us that it is a very useful and practical tool. By separating out the price effect, it allows the effects of other variables to show up more clearly. By its simplicity, it makes exploratory analysis easier to undertake. By forcing the analyst to spell out his assumptions, it leads to better *understanding* of how brands and markets work. But, over and above all this, the technique has two major practical applications.

Firstly, it makes it possible to measure advertising and other effects not only on sales volume but also on the price a brand can command. Advertising may be aiming to raise volume or to raise value (or indeed both). Both effects, therefore, need to be assessable together, which is what the demand curve method does.

Secondly, once a stable demand curve has been detected, it becomes a simple matter of plotting each month's new data on the graph in order to *monitor* the continuing progress of the brand. On-trend readings show stability. Off-trend readings quickly reveal that something is changing, and provide a basis for diagnosing the cause.

7
The Repositioning of Lucozade

BACKGROUND

While new product development work among marketeers often produces more excitement and effort, the successful repositioning of a well established brand is arguably a tougher job. For the company, financially it may be far more rewarding.

Lucozade is a glucose carbonated drink first made nearly 50 years ago. It is now marketed by Beecham Foods in the familiar dimpled 25 oz bottle with yellow cellophane wrap. The product is a highly concentrated source of energy, quickly assimilated into the bloodstream, it is easily digested, and its flavour, carbonation and relative sweetness make it easy to take in sickness.

This brand is a key source of profit to Beecham Foods and fluctuations in Lucozade volume and profit can radically affect the fortunes of the company.

THE PROBLEM

The period from 1974 to mid-1978 saw consistent volume decline. By mid-1978 it was clear that this was part of a long-term trend (Table 7.1). Leo Burnett and the Beecham brand group undertook a detailed analysis of all the possible causes of the situation. A brief review of the conclusions for each issue is made here.

TABLE 7.1: THE PROBLEM

Volume sales	Million doz.	% vs. last year
1974/5	3511	− 1.9
1975/6	3477	− 1.0
1976/7	3065	−11.8

Following four retail audit periods against Year Ago	
May/June	−17%
July/Aug	−16%
Sept/Oct	−22%
Nov/Dec	−15%

Illness

The brand history was steeped in illness/convalescence and so a close examination was made of the last ten years, on a monthly basis, of the relationship of volume sales to the levels of illness, as supplied by the Department of Health and Social Security.

The result of this analysis showed that there were fewer flu epidemics and a trend to lower illness levels generally – a healthier population. Peaks of illness and epidemics provided only 'cream' on the top of the volume sales trend. Levels of illness did not affect the fundamental shape and size of the trend.

Changing Consumer Attitudes

The housewife had been through four to five years of trauma in the high street: raging inflation and a shrinking purse. A new, more cautious housewife emerged from this period with a changing set of values which included an increasing degree of cynicism towards para-medical products. The effect of this trend alone on Lucozade was no more severe than for other products in similar fields. However, when taken in conjunction with the next factor of price, it was producing an effect.

Price

A careful examination was made comparing the reaction of volume sales to price movements over a ten year period. Until 1976 the rate of increase in Lucozade price had remained below the rise in the Retail Price Index. Since the beginning of 1976, Lucozade price increases had moved ahead of the Retail Price Index (Table 7.2). Lucozade was coming under severe scrutiny by the housewife in her new consciousness of price/value relationships.

TABLE 7.2: LUCOZADE RECOMMENDED RETAIL PRICING HISTORY
(DEFLATED BY THE RPI TO 1970 PRICES)

Year	Prices in pence[a]
69/70	16.1
70/71	16.0
71/72	15.3
72/73	15.5
73/74	13.4
74/75	12.7
75/76	12.3
76/77	12.4
77/78	12.9
78/79 (forecast)	13.0

[a] Excluding bottle deposit.

Retail Distribution

Twenty per cent of Lucozade volume is sold through chemists and 80 per cent through grocers. However, Lucozade's grocery trading profile was not following the same pattern as other major food and drink brands. One would normally hope to see at least 40 per cent of volume coming from the dynamic and rapidly growing multiple sector. In Lucozade's case this was only 20 per cent, with the remaining grocery volume coming from symbol groups and independents.

Although clearly not the major cause for any volume decline, this was identified as a concerning situation.

Sales Force

Sales force attention is traditionally concentrated on areas of high volume and excitement and for the Beecham Foods sales force this was provided by an extensive range of canned and bottled soft drinks. Lucozade, on the other hand, although much more profitable to the company than soft drinks, sold very much lower volumes and generated very little excitement. The consequence of this was a lack of real sales force attention.

Advertising

There were two parts to this analysis: spend levels and copy.

The analysis of advertising spend showed all the hallmarks of a series of short-term actions being taken in order to achieve fiscal profit targets. In the short term, price had eased upwards, profit had eased upwards, advertising spend had declined – and the brand volume had declined.

The company had maintained short-term profit by pushing pricing while jeopardizing the future growth of the brand. Since 1973, real advertising weight had been reduced by nearly half (Table 7.3).

TABLE 7.3: ADVERTISING WEIGHT AND VOLUME SALES (EX-FACTORY).
INDEX[a]: 1970=100

	Advertising	Volume sales
1973/4	129	123
1974/5	121	121
1975/6	96	120 (flu)
1976/7	70	105
1977/8	77	116 (flu)
1978/9	52	110

[a] Expressed as equivalent TVRs.

The copy analysis was equally revealing. For 12 years there had been a remarkable consistency in advertising strategy and execution. It showed slice-of-life situations promoting Lucozade as a unique source of liquid energy that helps the family when they are recovering from illness. In every execution, the emotional way of showing the family was through children.

The result of this was that while few brands in the marketplace could claim to have such a spontaneously strong and clear image, the brand was increasingly seen as being for sickness only, for kids only, for occasional use.

THE SOLUTION

It was clear, therefore, that the problem was centred on the brand being driven into a tighter and tighter funnel. To build volume for the brand it was likely that a fresh positioning strategy would be necessary.

Concepts were drawn up to cover a spectrum of options ranging from the existing convalescence positioning to unashamed in-health consumption (Figure 7.1).

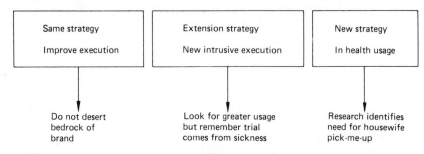

Figure 7.1

The results of a Usage and Attitude Study were analysed at this time, which helped to define the sample for the research which we were using to examine the strategy options.

More importantly, this Usage and Attitude Study revealed that only about 20 per cent of the volume of the brand was actually being used for straightforward convalescence and of the total volume only about 30 per cent was being used by children. A substantial volume of the product was being used in health and by adults (Table 7.4).

TABLE 7.4: PROPORTION OF CONSUMPTION AND PURPOSE

User	% Housewives	% Volume	Purpose
Heavy	5	50	Refreshing drink
Medium	9	32	Pick-me-up. Minor sickness.
Light	46	18	In sickness

The strategy research showed that heavy and medium purchasers, who represented the larger proportion of volume sales, approved the dramatic imagery move to in-health projection, while the light users understandably remained loyal to the sickness usage.

In addition this research and further qualitative work identified a clear need for a housewife pick-me-up during the day. While many products were already used for this purpose – tea, coffee, fruit juice, squash, Mars Bar, alcohol, etc. – there were problems associated with each of the options and it was felt that none would give, with such convenience and authority, the refreshing energy boost that was associated with Lucozade.

Summary of the Need for a Repositioning

1. Lucozade is strongly positioned for child sickness.
2. Child sickness is a highly limiting position in itself.
3. Child sickness is declining.
4. Less child sickness means less adult usage.

5. 100 per cent child convalescence copy does not stimulate adult usage.
6. Growth will come primarily from finding ways to stimulate new uses within the family.
7. New family uses must be approached cautiously in order not to destroy the current franchise.
8. Mother pick-me-up is the best opportunity to grow the business while maintaining the strength of the existing franchise.

ADVERTISING STRATEGY

It was determined therefore to reposition the brand to the consumer as a unique source of energy in health as well as in sickness. The importance of sickness remained as it provided tactical sales, would still be the reason for gaining new trial and would provide an authoritative rationale for any in-health message. Additionally, a sickness positioning being the bedrock of the brand keeps out competition.

But the thrust of the communication was now to be an in-health message.

It was recognized that a fine balance was required for communication success: no change was to be made to the product and at this stage, none to the packaging either. The only change would be advertising positioning and style. It was to be a tonal change for the brand, promoting an extension of usage. To push the brand too close to soft drinks would destroy the subtle imagery of Lucozade for ever and yet a distinctive change from its previous positioning must be clearly evident to the consumer.

The new *advertising objective* was simply to turn the brand from an occasional purchase into a more regular purchase. This was the key to building volume and persuading the growing end of the grocery trade to give Lucozade the support a major brand should have.

The *competitive positioning* of Lucozade would be that it is a unique source of energy in health as well as in sickness.

The *targeting* of the new advertising was crucial in that initially it was chosen to influence the softer options. The advertising would be targeted at the current heavy and medium purchasers.

Either they already used the brand as the advertising would demonstrate, in which case it provided justification for them for still further usage. Or they were purchasing it for their children while not drinking it themselves. In this case, the advertising would persuade them to use the product themselves whilst it was in the home. Either way, the advertising was targeted to housewives for self-consumption.

The proposition for such a brand as Lucozade must stem from something tangible within the product and something that is understood and relevant to the housewife. We had already established the need for a housewife pick-me-up during the day and this qualitative research had also clearly shown that glucose and energy were seen as synonymous. The message, therefore, was that Lucozade helped the body regain its normal energy level.

New Creative Strategy

Advertising Objective: To turn Lucozade from an occasional purchase into a more regular purchase.

Product Positioning: Lucozade is a unique source of energy in health as well as sickness.

Target Audience: Active women between the ages of 18 and 35 who care about the
                      health and well-being of themselves and their children.
Proposition: Lucozade helps the body regain its normal energy level.
Justification: Refreshing Lucozade is glucose energy in the most natural form
                      the body can use.
Tone: Contemporary, active, helpful, dependable, optimistic.

CREATIVE DEVELOPMENT

Early on in the rough executional development of the new strategy there emerged an 'energy
rate' idea which was felt to be so flexible and strong that it was agreed to execute this idea
in various ways for communication research.

The basic idea was that we all have an energy rate: when we are active this rate oscillates
vigorously; when we are tired, it is flat and depressed. This can be shown visually by an
oscillating coloured line.

Four treatments of this idea were created and animatics were made and put into communication research.

The route we chose was made into the commercial shown on p. 96. The reasons we opted for
this route were firstly, that the energy line was integrated into the action; it was in this
context that it was best liked and understood. Secondly, it showed everyday situations to
which the housewife could relate and it encouraged her to use the product frequently.

BUDGETS, MEDIA STRATEGY AND PLAN

It was accepted that one of the major causes of volume decline of the brand was the decline
in advertising weight. The decision was therefore taken to halt the decline in advertising to
sales ratio during the first 12 months after repositioning and then to reassess the situation.
This by no means represented a return to the previously high levels of advertising but
certainly represented reversal of a declining trend.

There had been a history of careful examination of media mix and deployment of funds
over time. The results of this had shown that Lucozade is highly sensitive to the weight of
TV advertising. Alternative media have not produced such an effect. In addition, past work
had shown that continuous advertising at low strike rates was more profitable than any other
deployment of funds.

While these issues were fully understood, it was recognized that the fresh positioning of
the brand required the housewife to see Lucozade in a new light and therefore media
planning had to play its part in creating a fresh boost for the brand.

Media Objectives

1. Create maximum awareness of new Lucozade usage opportunities as quickly as possible.
2. Maintain levels of awareness across the whole period.

Achievement of these objectives required a heavyweight burst pattern of TV at the start of
the repositioning. The TV weight dropped to under half the initial burst weight later on in
the plan, but was maintained over a longer period.

A women's press campaign began six months after the launch. This carried the traditional convalescence message to reinforce the roots of the brand, but in a media environment away from where we were concentrating the in-health advertising.

During the second half of the year posters were used to provide extra frequency of impact for the TV in-health message.

As the trade viewpoint was identified as a problem, a sales force and retail trade package was put together to tie-in with the new advertising:

On-pack promotion

Special 12 minute film for key account buyers

Special sales force material explaining the rationale for the change

Isolating the Advertising Influence

Although judgementally little else happened after the relaunch to change sales other than a fresh advertising approach, unquestionably other factors do affect the market. The problem is how to disentangle the influence of advertising from all the other factors. In order to make this assessment, the decision was made to leave the old convalescence advertising in the Tyne Tees area and use Beecham's Area Marketing Test Evaluation System (AMTES) to gauge what success the new advertising produced over what may have happened in the marketplace.

RESULTS

The task of changing people's perspective about a brand whose benefits and usage pattern were so well recognized cannot be achieved overnight. It was known from the outset that advertising repositioning was only the beginning of this task: if it appeared to have some tangible success, then other elements to accelerate the change would be brought to bear – pack sizes, labelling, PR, promotions, etc.

Advertising Research

The finished commercials, prior to airing on television, were researched by Beecham Foods in a quantified manner producing good results in terms of:

—communicating energy replacement in health,
—understanding the wavy line,
—liking the commercial,
—projected imagery.

Consumer Sales

The acid test of the strategy is its effect on sales in the marketplace after the launch of the new advertising. In sharp contrast to the previous severe volume decline of the brand, volume sales increased by 13 per cent in the first year.

Lucozade
Ups and Downs.

MAN: How often do you start out feeling full of get-up-and-go and then...

after you've been working hard, you start to slow down.

That's the time to sit down and have a glass of Lucozade. Lucozade's not just refreshing...

it provides glucose energy in the most natural form the body can use.

So, before you get up and get going again, have some Lucozade.

From the Lucozade television commercial.

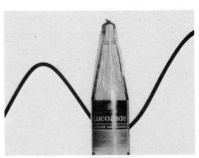

SINGERS: Lucozade refreshes you through the ups and downs of the day.

Isolating the Advertising Influence

It is unwise to attribute the sales increase entirely to the fresh advertising approach without further ado. Many things may influence sales.

The two principal scientific techniques that address this problem are market experimentation and econometric analysis. AMTES combines these two approaches in a computer model which utilizes the strength of both. The potential effects of many factors are removed by setting up an appropriately designed area test, an application of the experimental method of the natural sciences. The influences of the remaining factors that cannot be controlled in this way are measured and allowed for by AMTES in its calculation of the effect attributable to advertising. These measurements are derived from econometric analysis relating these factors to sales movements prior to the commencement of the area test.

The AMTES conclusion was that an 11 per cent volume sales increase was directly attributable to the change in advertising in the six months of the test. This should be compared with a volume sales increase of 21 per cent overall for the period of time. Clearly, nearly half of the sales increase observed was due to factors other than the change in advertising.

RELIABILITY OF THE AMTES RESULT

Because AMTES draws upon econometric analysis to arrive at its conclusions, it is subject to the caveats attendant upon the use of any statistical technique. Principally, the sales increase attributed to advertising is an estimate rather than an exact measurement. Other figures are possible, although of lower probability than the quoted estimate. AMTES provides a detailed analysis of the uncertainty attached to its calculations, which enables the user to assess the confidence that may be placed in them.

In this case, the analysis of the uncertainty associated with the best estimate of 11 per cent sales increase showed that the probability of a sales increase was 90 per cent. Put another way, there was a 90 per cent chance that the true sales change lay between the extremes of a 24 per cent sales increase and a 3 per cent sales decrease. Consequently, there was considerable confidence in the efficacy of the new advertising and it was introduced into Tyne Tees as well without further delay.

HOW AMTES WORKS

The objective of the econometric component of AMTES is to provide as good an estimate as possible of sales levels expected *if the area test had not been carried out*. Comparison of estimated with actual sales levels serves as the measure of the sales effect attributable to the test. In order to arrive at an estimate of expected sales levels, data for a period of time prior to the start of the test are analysed so as to explain sales movements in terms of market variables expected to influence sales. Actual values of these market variables during the test can then be used in the econometric model to produce the required sales estimates. The statistical quality of this model provides the basis on which the associated analysis of uncertainty is erected.

Operationally, fluctuations in the ratio of sales in the test area to those in the control area during the pretest period (March/April 1973 to May/June 1978 in this case) are related to similar ratios for the market variables. Subject to data availability, many market variables can be submitted to the AMTES programme, but not all will necessarily explain sales movements, e.g. some may not have changed much over the duration of the pretest period. AMTES uses a multiple linear regression procedure which examines all of the submitted market variables singly and in all combinations so as to choose automatically just that combination which best explains the observed sales ratio fluctuations, subject to the statistical quality of the chosen model being satisfactory.

For this AMTES analysis, all of the submitted variables were chosen for inclusion in the selected model. These were:

1. Lucozade sterling distribution.
2. Lucozade average retail price.
3. Lucozade advertising weight (in TVRs).
4. Sickness levels (new claims to sickness benefit).
5. Dummy variable to account for the change in the Nielsen retail audit universe in 1975.

These variables contributed nearly half of the observed sales increase, the remainder being attributed to the change in advertising platform (note that the effects of advertising *weight* are not included in the advertising effect of an 11 per cent sales increase).

Clearly, the fairly common practice of evaluating area tests in terms simply of sales changes on a year ago is totally inadequate and is likely to be highly misleading.

Usage and Attitude

Following the repositioning advertising, a regular Usage and Attitude Study went into the field. While no dramatic results were expected at an early stage, a number of movements in a positive direction were recorded:

(a) A significant increase in claiming to buy Lucozade 'nowadays'.
(b) A significant increase in strong likelihood of 'ever buyers' to repurchase.
(c) A significant increase in claims to purchase Lucozade for 'refreshment' reasons among frequent purchasers.
(d) A significant increase in the recall of Lucozade television advertising.

CONCLUSIONS

Old product development requires skilful balancing. The old consumer franchise is vital, the new consumer franchise is the future life blood of the brand. This case history demonstrates how advertising can play the key role in revitalizing an established brand of great importance which had been in severe volume decline. This is not just a case of one campaign being better than the previous one but the development of more productive, better quality, more relevant advertising, building sales to provide the funds for renewed investment in the brand, which in turn will stimulate future growth.

8
Shloer

Increase in Sales as a Result of a Media Change

INTRODUCTION

Shloer Apple and Grape Juices are marketed in Britain by Beecham Foods. The advertising for this brand has been handled since 1974 by J. Walter Thompson and, until 1978, all advertising appeared in press.

In 1977, the performance of the brand, in terms of distribution and sales, and consumer awareness of the brand, were reviewed. For reasons which are detailed below, it was agreed that a TV commercial should be tested in the STAGS TV area, during the latter part of 1978, and sales monitored by the Beecham AMTES model. On the basis of the results in Scotland, a decision would be made as to whether to extend TV advertising to the rest of the country.

The results of the test were so positive that it has been agreed to extend advertising on TV to other parts of the country as soon as possible. The extension of the campaign was planned for 1979, but was thwarted by the TV strike. The campaign will therefore be extended from June 1980.

One of the major conditions for extending the campaign was that advertising should be financed by the brand with no additional investment made by Beecham Foods. In order to adhere to this, the extension of the advertising has been planned as a roll-out, starting with areas of strength. Scotland is the brand's strongest area, which is why it was chosen for the test. That a change in media strategy can affect awareness of the brand and generate new sales, thus enabling the brand to finance further support and create further growth, is the main argument of this paper.

CONCLUSIONS

1. The TV test conducted in the STAGS area for Shloer had the effect of increasing sales at a 99.9 per cent level of confidence.
2. The increase in sales, at a 95 per cent level of confidence, was between 20 and 63 per cent. The most probable increase was 45 per cent. A 21 per cent increase was needed to break even on the advertising investment.
3. That advertising was directly responsible for this increase is the conclusion which can

be drawn from the Beecham AMTES model. The effects of price and distribution both for Shloer and the main competitor, Bulmers, and the effect of temperature, are discounted by this model as being insignificant.

4. In addition, awareness and penetration of Shloer increased in the test area, as measured by a pre- and post-check.

5. Sufficient funds have been generated by the STAGS test to justify rolling-out a television campaign across the rest of the country.

BACKGROUND: THE BRAND PRIOR TO THE TV TEST

Advertising History

Shloer Apple Juice was introduced into the UK in 1946 by H. W. Carter & Co. In 1961, the manufacturing, selling and distribution rights were bought by Beecham Foods.

The brand has been advertised in press for many years, but in 1974, when the account moved to JWT, a new campaign was developed which ran consistently until 1977 in black and white and in 1977 in colour. The campaign entitled 'Shloer and the Family', of which examples are included, appeared in the Sunday press.

Awareness of Shloer's advertising and of the brand itself was very low even among the target group of BC1 housewives, aged 20-45. A 1976 Usage and Attitude Study, which was conducted after the black and white campaign had run for two years, showed that only 54 per cent of the sample (which was drawn from the target group) had heard of Shloer, and of these only 34 per cent claimed awareness of the advertising. Only 29 per cent of those aware of Shloer who also read the media schedule recognized an example of the campaign. Clearly the advertising lacked impact.

It was lack of impact which first led Beechams to consider increasing the advertising budget in 1977-78. A translation of the existing campaign into half-page colour using the same schedule as before was agreed. Meanwhile plans for the development of a TV commercial went ahead.

Sales and Distribution

Since Beecham Foods relaunched the brand in 1968 into its distinctive green, wine-shaped bottle, sales of Shloer have shown steady growth, though from a very small base. In spite of low levels of awareness the brand's volume was increasing year on year, which gave Beecham and JWT the basis for optimism concerning the possible effect of a more impactful advertising campaign (Table 8.1).

The introduction of the grape variant in 1973-74 gave the brand extra sales, and grape now accounts for half of total Shloer sales in some areas of the country. Nevertheless, apple, too, increased its sales slowly. The very hot summers of 1975 and 1976 gave rise to increases in total sales year on year of 40 per cent, and although the brand lost volume in 1977-78, sales did not decline to their pre-1975 levels, thus indicating either an increase in frequency of purchase among existing users or an increase in the number of loyal users who were converted by trial during hot summers. Either way, the signs were optimistic.

The brand has suffered, however, from low levels of distribution. In 1974 sterling distribution was 53 per cent nationally, by 1978 it was still only 54 per cent. There were massive variations by region in both sales per head of population and distribution.

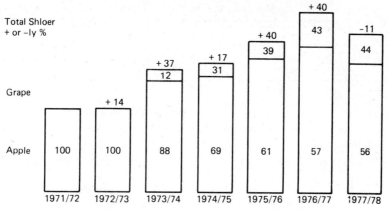

TABLE 8.1: SHLOER SALES: APPLE AND GRAPE (%) (NIELSEN)

As can be seen from Table 8.2, the sales indices and levels of distribution are closely aligned: in general, with Southern the exception, the stronger the distribution, the better are the sales. The need to persuade the trade to stock Shloer is clear – and a powerful argument in favour of stocking a brand is often the fact that the brand is receiving strong advertising support.

TABLE 8.2: TOTAL SHLOER SALES AND DISTRIBUTION PRE-TV TEST

	% sales	% population	Sales index 1977/78	% £ distribution at DJ 1978
Scotland	16	8.4	196	71
London	27	21.2	127	62
Yorks	10	10.0	100	54
Anglia	6	5.9	98	53
Tyne Tees	5	5.2	96	48
Southern	7	7.7	91	54
Lancs	12	13.3	90	43
W.W.W.	8	10.1	79	45
Midlands	9	14.9	60	46

Nielsen.

Competition

Shloer has one major competitor, Bulmers' Apple and Grape Juice. The brand is in even smaller distribution than is Shloer at around 25 per cent sterling, a level which, like Shloer, it has maintained without increase over a number of years. Bulmers have traditionally been strongest in the London area, with Scotland relatively weak.

In 1975 and 1976 Bulmers conducted a TV test in the London area, like Shloer following a strategy which capitalized on areas of strength (Table 8.3).

However, there has been no further advertising support of any kind for the brand since 1976 and we assume that the decision to discontinue the test results from there having been no apparent effect on sales. It is, of course, possible that, following the success of Shloer's advertising in Scotland, Bulmers may try again.

TABLE 8.3: BULMERS' TEST MARKET

	Expenditure £	Housewife TVRs	Coverage	OTS
1975 August	27 300	450	82	5.5
1976 May	51 400	700	87	8

MEAL and JWT estimates.

Although the total market increased when Bulmers entered in 1972 and has remained fairly steady since then, Bulmers share has declined (Table 8.4). The introduction of a grape variant in 1976 did little to improve Bulmers' position, as it obtained a 4 per cent share against Shloer's 96 per cent. All the growth in the grape market has come from Shloer.

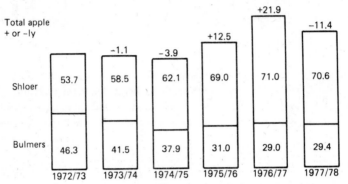

TABLE 8.4: SHLOER AND BULMERS' APPLE BRAND SHARES (NIELSEN)

Penetration and Frequency of Purchase

Like awareness, penetration and frequency of purchase for Shloer are very low. The 1976 Usage and Attitude Study measured penetration of the target group over twelve months as 22 per cent for Apple and 6 per cent for Grape. Only 20 per cent of those who bought Shloer Apple bought it once a month or more. The figure for Grape was slightly higher, at 31 per cent.

Seasonality

Shloer sales are highly seasonal, demonstrating regular sales peaks during the summer and at Christmas. Table 8.5 shows the seasonal pattern, averaged over four years.

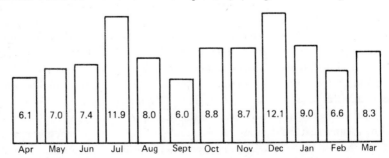

TABLE 8.5: AVERAGE MONTHLY SALES, AS A PERCENTAGE OF TOTAL ANNUAL SALES (BEECHAM STATISTICS)

Still from Shloer television advertisement: 'What more could a man ask for?'

Shloer press advertisement.

THE SHLOER TV TEST

Shloer's history pre-1978 had shown a steady increase in sales, from a very small base. It was, however, agreed that the brand could benefit not only from improved distribution, as those areas where the brand was strongest had better-than-average distribution already, but also from far greater awareness of the brand.

1978 Marketing Objectives

1. To increase profit margin.
2. To increase volume sales.

3. To broaden the consumer franchise by achieving substantial increase in penetration and frequency of purchase.
4. To increase Shloer's distribution within the grocery trade.

(for reasons of confidentiality, the actual levels of desired increase have been left out)

It was believed that increased investment in advertising would perform a major role in the achievement of the above objectives.

During 1978, therefore, the press campaign was continued nationally, still using the 'Shloer and the family' cartoon strip, in half-page colour in the three Sunday supplements. Colour was adopted as a means of improving visibility and impact.

But in the long term, it was agreed, greater investment was required if the above objectives were to be achieved.

It was decided that press could not achieve sufficient impact or visibility to promote the growth in trial which was needed if the brand were substantially to improve its consumer franchise, and it was therefore agreed to conduct a test in a different medium in one area, to see if a change in medium would effect a notable increase in consumer offtake.

Television was selected as the medium most likely to assist in the achievement of the above. It was believed that television advertising would

(a) offer a wider target audience
(b) give greater impact
(c) provide the trade with a reason to stock Shloer.

In the event of television advertising resulting in an increase in sales in the selected area, the campaign would be extended to other parts of the country.

The Selection of STAGS

Shloer is a small brand, and therefore cannot afford a large advertising budget. But more importantly, it was firmly believed by Beecham Foods that the brand should be self-supporting in all its advertising and promotional activity.

Television advertising at a national level was therefore unlikely to be affordable to Shloer for a number of years. A plan was therefore adopted whereby, in order eventually to fund TV advertising nationally, the advertising capitalized initially on areas of strength for the brand. Thus sufficient profit would be generated year by year to be able to afford to fund, as the campaign progressed, weaker areas, and eventually to sustain a national campaign.

STAGS has for many years been the area of greatest strength for Shloer, both in sales and distribution, and was therefore selected as being the most cost-effective area for a TV campaign, in terms of the likely return on investment to be expected from such a campaign. Equally, in the event of the campaign effecting no sales growth, or not enough to merit a continuation, the amount of money lost on such a test would be smaller in STAGS than in other areas of strength, such as London or Yorkshire.

Advertising Objectives

1. To increase sales of Shloer.
2. To increase awareness and penetration of Shloer among non-users in the target group.
3. To improve attitudes to Shloer among those already aware.

After evidence of success the campaign should extend into other areas of the country.

Target Group

The target group for the TV test was the same as that for the press campaign. It was defined as: 'Housewives, primarily those with a growing family, 25–45 years old, with middle-class values or aspirations.'

Creative Strategy

The creative strategy was simply a translation of the press campaign, the desired response to which was 'Shloer is a light, refreshing, natural drink, to be drunk whenever the whole family is together.'

It was important that the creative strategy did not change, as the test was of the media strategy.

Media Strategy

The media selection was dictated by the nature of the test, as was the selected area.

The 30 second commercial 'Thankful' was aired in STAGS for a total of ten weeks. This was broken into three bursts in June, August and December, to cover the main sales peaks of the year. Net expenditure was £21 700, which delivered a total of 1170 housewife TVRs, 90 per cent coverage, and 13 average OTS.

EVALUATING THE CAMPAIGN

Sales Increases

In order to evaluate the effect of the TV campaign on sales of Shloer, a total of 27 Nielsen periods were used to record consumer sales, from December/January 1974 to April/May 1979. Nielsen data were recorded in both test and control areas.

The earliest 21 periods (up to and including April/May 1978) will be referred to as the pretest period. The six periods from June/July 1978 to April/May 1979 are considered to be the test period, as they cover one year's sales from the start of TV advertising in June 1978.

The simplest way of looking at these data is to compare percentage changes year-on-year in sales in both the test and control areas, using an annual average.

As can be seen from Table 8.6, annual levels of growth were declining in the test area for the three years prior to the TV test. During the test period, however, sales in the test area increased by 24 per cent on the previous year, whereas in the rest of the country they continued to decline.

A further way of examining the effect of the test is to look at the share of sales which

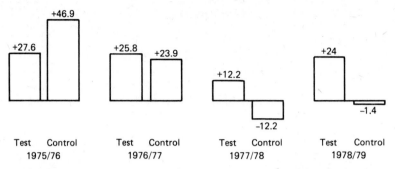

TABLE 8.6: PERCENTAGE CHANGES IN SALES YEAR-ON-YEAR (YEAR BEGINNING JUNE/JULY) (NIELSEN)

existed in Scotland against the share in the rest of the country. The graph in Table 8.7 shows Scotland's share both during the pretest and the test periods. Up to June 1978, the share was relatively stable, with the exception of two sharp increases in share which occurred during the summer and Christmas periods in 1977–78. However, looked at as an annual average on the same basis as Table 8.6, Scotland increased its share of Shloer sales during the test period by 27 per cent on the previous year.

Expressed as a sales index against the rest of the country (on the same basis as in Table 8.2), Shloer's index in Scotland increased from 196 in 1977–78 to 202 in 1978–79:

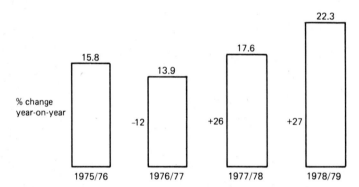

TABLE 8.7: SCOTLAND'S SHARE OF SHLOER SALES (YEAR BEGINNING JUNE/JULY) (NIELSEN)

The AMTES Evaluation of Sales

In addition to the above analysis of sales and share increase, the Beecham AMTES Model (Area Marketing Test Evaluation System) was used, in order to ascertain the exact levels of increase which could be attributed to use of advertising, and in order to screen from the analysis the other variables which might have affected sales in the test area.

The specific purpose of the Beecham AMTES model is to measure *the effect of advertising on sales*. In order to do this, any variables which are likely to affect sales, other than the advertising, are introduced into the computer alongside the sales data for both test and control areas. In the case of Shloer, the variables which were included as likely to affect sales were:

Price   — Shloer
                  — Bulmers
Distribution   — Shloer
                  — Bulmers

Temperature (included because of the highly seasonal nature of sales which increase during summer and at Christmas).

According to AMTES, the effect of the variables of price, distribution and temperature were so small as to be almost totally insignificant, and any increases or decreases in sales in the test area, both during and prior to the advertising, could not be attributed to any of these. The increases, therefore, which have already been noted in the test area during the test period, can, according to the AMTES model, be attributed only to the advertising. Figure 8.1 shows how actual sales increased against a straight line which AMTES projected

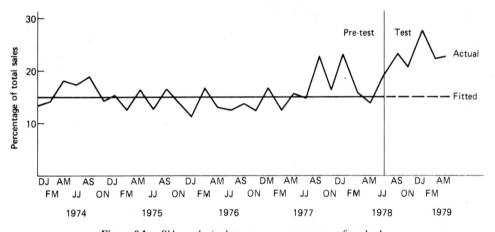

Figure 8.1.   *Shloer sales in the test area as a percentage of total sales.*

as being the likely progress of sales had the advertising not occurred, calculated on the performance of the brand during the 21 pretest Nielsen periods.

Although, as can be observed from the graph, sales during the summer and Christmas periods in 1977–78 had increased against the previous years' peaks, the overall increase in sales for that year was far smaller than for 1978–79 – the dips between the seasonal peaks were much less marked during the test period. The AMTES analysis demonstrated not only that sales were up 24 per cent on the previous year, and the share up by 27 per cent, but also that *the advertising* accounted for an increase in sales of between 28 and 63 per cent. This was based on the straight-line projection from the data of the previous four years and the state of sales in the control area, which, as has already been demonstrated, were in decline, and this analysis of the advertising contribution was projected at a 95 per cent level of confidence.

The most probable increase in sales in the test area resulting purely from the advertising is, according to AMTES, 45 per cent. This presupposes a probable decline in sales in line with the rest of the country had the advertising not occurred.

In order to break-even against the advertising investment, an increase of 21 per cent in sales was required. This was calculated on the basis of how much extra profit needed to be generated in order to cover the cost of TV airtime. In fact, it would appear that the test not only broke even but was profitable, and the possibility of extending the test to other areas was thus feasible. The marketing objectives of increasing profit margins and volume sales were met in the test area, and the foundations laid for meeting the longer-term objectives of increase in distribution, penetration and frequency of purchase.

Meeting the objectives of increased awareness and penetration

In addition to the AMTES analysis, a pre- and post-awareness and penetration check was carried out in Scotland. The pre-test was conducted between 26th June and 5th July, and the post-test after two bursts from 25th September to 4th October, using a sample of 500 women throughout the STAGS area.

Total awareness of Shloer rose from 36 per cent to 51 per cent post advertising. Increase was noted in particular among the 15–54 age groups (Table 8.8).

Penetration of Shloer rose from 23 to 30 per cent, again the main increases being in the 15–54 age group (Table 8.9).

Immediately after the TV advertising in STAGS during the summer of 1978, we saw an increase in both awareness and penetration of Shloer, and were thus confident that the second of the advertising objectives had been met.

TABLE 8.8: TOTAL AWARENESS OF SHLOER BY AGE

		Total	15–34	35–54	55+
June	%	36	46	33	27
September	%	51	66	56	34

Beecham/Systems 3.

TABLE 8.9: PURCHASE OF SHLOER (EVER BOUGHT)

		Total	15–34	35–54	55+
June	%	23	27	23	18
September	%	30	37	33	21

Beecham/Systems 3.

EXTENDING THE CAMPAIGN

Because Scotland is the strongest area for Shloer sales, it was possible not only to break even, but to create substantial profit during the test period. The AMTES analysis concluded that the chances of achieving break-even nationally during the same period would be about 3 in 20, as an increase of 55 per cent in volume sales would be required. However, by taking one area at a time, working through areas of strength and maintaining the campaign in Scotland, it would be possible to generate sufficient funds for a roll-out across the country. This strategy has been adopted, and commenced in June 1980.

9

Swan Vesta Matches

BUSINESS BACKGROUND

In 1975, the situation facing Bryant & May in the UK match market was a less than encouraging one. The market had been steadily declining for 15 years, in which time it had lost a quarter of its volume. Bryant & May was the leading manufacturer with about half of the £43m market. Its volume, however, had declined faster than the market despite an annual expenditure on advertising of £250 000. Bryant & May was losing share to cheaper, imported matches which sold in multiwraps and undercut its trade price by as much as 20 per cent.

The following case history illustrates how the company arrested this decline by identifying the markets in which it was operating more accurately and by promoting more effectively against its existing strengths.

Matches compete in the lights market against various forms of mechanical lighter. 'Lights' are match marketing terminology for acts of ignition and in 1975 the lights market constituted 224 billion lights – of which 40 per cent were matches. This match share had fallen in volume terms by 27 per cent since 1960, in spite of an increase in *total* lights – an expansion which was more than absorbed by lighter sales, and, in particular, by sales of disposable lighters.

The lights market comprises lights used for smoking (70 per cent of all lights) and those used for domestic purposes.

In the smoking market, the company's main competitors – lighters – had been heavily advertised over the previous decade not only as a means of obtaining a light, but also as an object which signalled social distinction. Matches were increasingly seen as the poor man's alternative.

MARKETING AND ADVERTISING OBJECTIVES

The company identified as its main objective the need to reverse the trend whereby matches were losing share of the lights market. This would be accomplished by creating a consumer brand franchise for match brands in order to develop sales volume profitably.

The first step was clearly to establish the perceived strengths and weaknesses of the product in the consumer's mind.

Qualitative attitude research showed matches to have considerable latent appeal. They were seen as a natural, readily available commodity; a traditional part of our way of life; a completely reliable source of a light. Lighters were seen as expensive, easy to lose, and, most importantly to smokers, liable to break down or run out of fuel or flint.

Distinctions between brands of matches were minimal. Only Swan Vesta was seriously seen as a branded product worth asking for by name.

An NOP survey into the usage of matches for smoking showed that nearly one third of smokers (31 per cent) alternated between matches and lighters, seeing each as more appropriate on different occasions. Qualitative research expanded upon this information, showing that it would be harder to persuade the 44 per cent of smokers who used only a lighter to use matches than it would to persuade those who already used both to use more matches.

On the basis of this information Bryant & May constructed its strategy on the smoking market. It was decided to put the main thrust of the promotional support behind the one national brand – Swan. The qualities latent in the brand were the essential qualities which made the case for matches against lighters. Swan matches were reliable because they were a traditional quality match, well made and well packed. This was the focus of the attack on lighters: 'The unreliable light'.

But this was not a claim which offered much promise at a rational level, as it was battling against a lot of carefully constructed unconscious associations for lighters, built up by advertising over a considerable period.

Lighters were 'socially superior'.

SWAN CAMPAIGN 1976-1979: CREATIVE STRATEGIES AND EXECUTIONS

On being appointed in mid-1975, the agency, with the company's help, formulated a creative strategy for Swan which homed in on the chief virtue of matches – their reliability – and claimed it both for Swan and for the Swan user. The strategy adhered to over this four year campaign from 1976 to 1979 is reproduced below:

Advertising Strategy

The problem the advertising should address: Matches are seen as socially inferior to lighters. Smokers need to be reassured that Swan is acceptable in any company.

The people the advertising should reach: All smokers who use matches.

What the advertising should aim to achieve: To position Swan as the match that one can use anywhere.

What the advertising should say: Swan is a really reliable match, so you can depend on Swan not to let you down.

Tone of voice in advertisement: Will complement the brand image by being masculine, contented and relaxed.

The advertising for Swan took on the lighter one-upmanship instilled through past advertising for lighters by depicting social occasions of offering a light for smoking, where the lighter lost its superficial glamour by failing to produce a light, and where the Swan user took over the situation.

The advertising was constructed to bring out the qualities discovered from research to be associated both with the Swan user – the 'strong, silent type' – and with the product itself, i.e. *reliability*.

Cowboy.

Prisoner of War.

Bunker.

Husband.

K6.

Stills from Swan Vesta television advertisements 1976–78.

"It's nice to know there's something you can rely on–Swan."

The theme of the campaign, showing the product in its social role, and briefly demonstrating the comparison with other lights, demanded television.

In addition, the medium was needed for its ability to deliver modernity and urgency – necessary for what is essentially a low-interest product with an old-fashioned, downmarket image. The credibility of a highly visible TV campaign was required.

Five situations were used to create 30 second commercials with the common theme: '*It's nice to know there's something you can rely on – Swan*'.

In each case, the 'Swan man' user is dependable and mature and in complete control of the situation in which he finds himself. He uses Swan with quiet confidence when more flashy individuals with mechanical lighters fail to produce a light.

MEDIA STRATEGY AND PLANS

The prime marketing objective of the Swan Vesta campaign was to stem the flow of light sales from matches to lighters, and, more specifically, to halt the decline in Swan Vesta sales. This would be accomplished through improving feeling towards the brand amongst the target audience by building positive attitudes in the dimensions of reliability, quality and suitability for use anywhere.

A regular pattern of advertising was, therefore, felt to be the most important consideration. Awareness of Swan Vesta as shown by NOP data (see Table 9.1) was already very high, and the secondary objective was maintaining this high level.

The media strategy and planning was biased towards male smokers, who made up a high proportion of the 'sometimes use matches' smokers. The committed Swan man was traditionally very loyal so the main purpose of the commercials was to reassure occasional users that Swan was worth buying more often.

Research and judgement backed the feeling that young smokers under 25 years were very fickle in their lighting habits and that people tended to mature into Swan usage. Thus, in age terms the media planning bias was to mature, stable individuals under 45, as it was felt to be extremely difficult to change the associated smoking habits of older regular smokers.

Post analysis of the results of the first series of television bursts indicated the optimum pattern of advertising to be 400–450 TVRs over four weeks followed by an eight-week gap.

Television advertising commenced in April 1976 with a four-week national burst followed by further bursts in June/July and August/September 1976. This pattern of advertising was continued up until March 1979 as funds allowed.

Although the initial objective had been to advertise nationally at the optimum TVR level, insufficient funds made it necessary to drop regions from the schedule for some of the bursts. This was judged preferable to continuing to advertise nationally at a less effective weight.

CAMPAIGN EVALUATION

In the three financial years 1976–78, Bryant & May spent a total of £1 118 006 on regular Swan advertising. Clearly, at this level of commitment it is essential to be assured that the expenditure is productive.

A statistical project to evaluate the effects of Swan advertising on actual sales – rather

TABLE 9.1: SPONTANEOUS AWARENESS/PROMPTED AWARENESS OF SWAN VESTA

	Jul 75	Oct 75	Jan 76	Mar 76	Oct 76	Mar 77	Mar 78	Oct 78	Oct 78[a]
Total	75/96	69/96	65/94	73/96	72/93	72/92	75/95	77/98	80/100
Scotland	86/98	75/97	69/96	77/97	72/96	70/89	76/92	83/97	82/100
North	75/95	67/95	65/96	74/97	74/92	78/95	79/96	76/98	82/100
Mid/W.W/E. Ang	76/97	69/96	65/93	72/97	75/95	70/92	75/95	78/97	82/100
London	75/97	68/96	63/91	68/92	64/93	67/90	68/94	76/99	79/99
S/S. West	65/96	70/95	64/94	73/95	71/92	71/92	76/96	74/98	79/99

NOP Match Survey – all adults.
[a] All smokers.

than merely on image and awareness – was embarked upon. The project examined the differences made by varying weights of advertising by area on an annual financial year basis for the three years 1976, 1977 and 1978, when a relatively stable pattern of regular Swan advertising was adhered to.

Due to budget cuts it was not possible to run national advertising over this three-year period. The result was regional variations in the weight of advertising. It was aimed to hold at least one area as a control with a regular pattern of advertising; this area was Yorkshire. The areas with the next highest weights of advertising were, in descending order: London, Tyne Tees, Lancashire and Midlands (Table 9.2).

TABLE 9.2: TV RATING POINTS FOR SWAN VESTA

Adult TVR	1976	1977	1978	Total
London	1077	1215	1554	3846
Southern	1016	0	769	1785
Harlech	979	0	0	979
Midland	1031	1009	432	2472
Lancs	1090	1088	511	2689
Yorks	1074	3042	1503	5619
Tyne Tees	1074	1745	427	3246
Scotland	1017	1219	0	2236

Over this three-year period all other marketing activity was constant, with no real peaks of promotional activity in any areas or at any special time. There were also no major competitive launches in the smoking match area. The launch of Winners occurred in 1979.

The evaluation of regional advertising effects on Swan sales at different exposure weights was then calculated. The areas were listed in order of the total TV rating points achieved over this three-year period and compared with the Nielsen regional Swan volume sales increase over the same period (Table 9.3).

TABLE 9.3: EFFECT OF TV ADVERTISING ON SWAN VESTA SALES VOLUME, 1976–78

	Adult TVR	Volume index
Yorks	5619	117
London	3846	113
Tyne Tees	3246	112
Lancs	2689	110
Midland	2472	111
Scotland	2236	98
Southern	1785	108
Harlech	979	101

Volume index = Nielsen Match Swan volume, 1978 indexed on 1976.
N.B. Anglia is not shown owing to non-availability of Nielsen data for the early part of the period 1976–78.

The result was an extremely positive correlation between the amount of sales increase and the advertising weight per area (Figure 9.1).

The only aberration was Scotland, which had a medium weight of advertising and Swan sales did not increase. This can be explained by the fact that Bluebell – 'the only Scottish match' – was advertised and strongly promoted during this period.

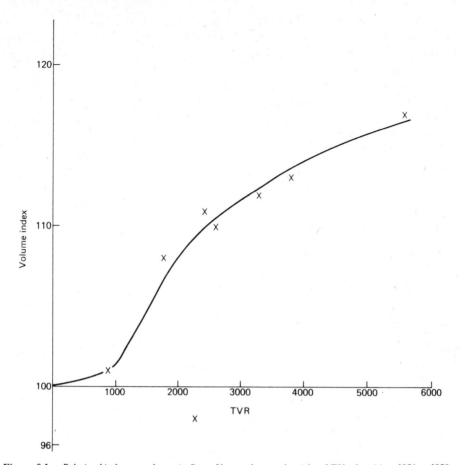

Figure 9.1. *Relationship between change in Swan Vesta volume and weight of TV advertising, 1976 to 1978.*

Yorkshire, the area with the highest TVR total – 5619 – achieved a sales increase of 17 per cent while Harlech, with the lowest level at 979 TVRs, experienced only a 1 per cent gain. Each area, apart from Scotland, was correlated well in descending order.

It is not only these increases in the sales of Swan Vesta which demonstrate the effectiveness of the campaign 1976–78. Over this period, against a history of decline, matches consistently increased their share of smoking lights at the expense of all other lights (Table 9.4).

TABLE 9.4: THE SMOKING LIGHTS MARKET, 1975–78

	Smoking lights 000m	Matches 000m	Matches index	% share	Lighters 000m	Lighters index	% share	Disposable lighters 000m	% share
1975	156.2	62.8	100	40.2	93.4	100	59.8		
1976	154.1	63.6	101	41.2	86.0	92	55.8	4.5	2.9
1977	149.2	65.7	105	44.0	77.0	82	51.6	6.5	4.4
1978	147.8	66.3	106	44.9	72.3	77	48.9	9.2	6.2

Source: Bryant & May.

CONCLUSION

The data presented above are strong evidence for a relationship between advertising and sales response and for the effectiveness of the Swan Vesta campaign 1976–78 as the cornerstone of the marketing policy for the brand.

Marketing rarely has the opportunity of working in perfect conditions; it is not a science. It is in essence the art of managing limited resources in an imperfect, real world. The reason for claiming that the strategy adopted since 1976 is a proven success is that Bryant & May has addressed its real problems – a shrinking market and a declining share of smoking lights – and has reversed both these trends. Its marketing strategy is established and on course, and the foundations are secured for further development.

10
An Evaluation of the Effectiveness of the Current Campari Campaign

'How can you possibly. . .?'
'Like this mate!'

INTRODUCTION

Coinciding with a new advertising campaign, Campari's volume sales increased by a remarkable 62 per cent between 1976 and 1980. This case history will show the vital role that an integrated advertising strategy, in terms of planning input, media choice and creative content, played in that growth. It will seek to demonstrate a causal relationship between advertising and Campari sales performance, and the success of the campaign in achieving its objectives of broadening out the brand and making it a more enjoyable drink.

BACKGROUND

1976 was a turning point for Campari and its advertising. It was the year when Findlater Matta and the Agency decided that Campari should descend from its pedestal. The carefully planned national roll-out had been completed the previous year, so there were no more easy regional gains to be made. The rapid sales growth which the brand had enjoyed since the mid-60s was slowing down. Neither was Campari's position helped by the depression of the drinks market generally. The end of the consumer boom checked the expansion of whisky, gin, white rum and wines. Only vodka, vermouth and lager succeeded in bucking the trend, and all three owed their resilience, in part at least, to the support of younger drinkers. By the mid-70s, therefore, Campari needed a fresh impetus, and advertising, as we will demonstrate, had a key part to play.

Fortunately, Campari had already shown itself to be responsive to advertising. The cryptically bitter, distinctively pink drink had established itself, with the help of ingenious, sophisticated, witty and highly original advertising, and despite a modest budget, as a smart, elitist brand. Advertising had helped to create a 'larger than life' personality for Campari over and above its idiosyncratic physical attributes. The product itself was used to breaking all the rules – absurdly conspicuous in colour and far too bitter for the average taste – and advertising had added style, humour, status and exclusivity. There was a danger, however, that Campari might have become too esoteric and narrow in its appeal.

FACTORS AFFECTING PLANNING A NEW CAMPAIGN

Two key factors lay behind the planning for a new Campari advertising campaign:

The Need to Expand Brand Usership

Campari had set out deliberately to attract adventurous and discriminating drinkers. They were a minority of discoverers who enjoyed flaunting their sophistication, and took pride in the knowledge that Campari did not appeal to all tastes.

The brand's user profile was upmarket and slightly older. Unfortunately, an ageing, middle class market, vulnerable to the effects of inflation and recession, did not provide sufficient scope for Campari's ambition for volume.

Campari needed to achieve a more stable and democratic base. This meant recruiting new, younger, mass market trialists from among the socially mobile, high-spending, heavier drinkers with the discretionary income to spend drinking in pubs in the evenings.

The Need to Increase Product Acceptability

For over one hundred years, soda had always been accepted as the mixer for Campari, and in the UK, for fourteen years, soda had been advertised as the only mixer. The bitterness of Campari and soda had marked it as a specialist and acquired taste.

Product tests conducted late in 1975 showed that, as far as adult drinkers generally were concerned, other mixers performed better than soda both in terms of expectations and trial (Table 10.1).

TABLE 10.1: APPEAL OF MIXERS FOR CAMPARI

	Pre-trial: Expect to like very much %	Post-trial: Like very much %
Lemonade	37	25
Tonic	17	25
Bitter lemon	17	26
Soda	17	17

Martin Hamblin Research, October 1975.

The sweetness of these mixers vis-à-vis soda tended to offset Campari's bitterness and give them a wider appeal. Campari and lemonade, in particular, looked promising.

THE ADVERTISING SOLUTION

Strategic Aims

The campaign objectives were twofold:

(i) To open up the brand, preserving the originality, humour and style that had attracted early converts, but developing an identity that would appeal to new, younger recruits;

(ii) To encourage people to drink Campari in any way they found enjoyable.

Target Audience

The target group included both:

(i) Traditional, slightly older, upmarket Campari users loyal to soda.

(ii) Experienced, younger, mass-market drinkers who might be interested in experimenting with other mixers.

They were defined as confident drinkers, more sophisticated and sceptical about drinks and their advertising, and therefore likely to be susceptible to communications that were commensurately more innovative, difficult and demanding.

Still from Campari television advertisement: 'How could you possibly...?' 'Like this mate.'

Target Responses

These were the responses which we wished to elicit from our advertising:

1. *From the senses*
—conspicuously, beautifully pink
—refreshingly bitter

2. *From the reason*
—enjoyable whatever you choose to drink it with, but especially with soda or lemonade

3. *From the emotions*
—stylish, irreverent, arrogant, surprising
—not afraid of sending itself up or breaking rules
—a badge for the more individualistic, experienced, demanding and exhibitionist drinker
   to wear

The Creative Execution

The creative solution balanced an appeal to the new, younger, brasher Campari trialist with reassurance for the Campari and soda establishment. It set out to shock and surprise younger drinkers, to force them to take notice of Campari by behaving differently from other brands of drinks.

The advertising depicted a contrast of styles in an enigmatic encounter between a mature and sophisticated Campari and soda traditionalist and a self-confident, beautiful Cockney girl drinking Campari with lemonade. Each embodied values which one part of the target audience could identify with. Neither side won exactly, but it was the unknown Cockney girl - Lorraine Chase - who captured the popular imagination.

In addition to soda, we elected to focus on one specific new mixer - lemonade - rather than a mixer versatility story, which other drinks had told already. As an added bonus, lemonade had the widest distribution in the drinks trade, and was even served free like soda in some parts of the country. It also made a pretty drink, as colourful and distinctive as Campari and soda.

The first television commercial went on the air during the week commencing 24th May 1976. The campaign was still running in 1980.

Media Strategy

Since 1970, Campari had been advertised nationally in magazines and regionally on television. As we were trying to modify existing attitudes and behaviour rather sharply, we wanted to use a medium capable of making an immediate impact. We also wanted a more public medium appropriate to our wider target audience.

Although the bulk of advertising in 1975 had been in the press, we decided to return to television in 1976. Television had already played an important part in the successful extension of Campari during the roll-out, not only among consumers but also with the trade.

The majority of the budget between 1976 and 1980 was spent on television and in summer advertising bursts.

CAMPAIGN EVALUATION

Since 1975, Campari's volume sales have grown impressively by 62 per cent; lemonade has been established as an alternative mixer to soda; more younger recruits have joined the brand; the award-winning campaign has become famous, talked about and copied; and 'The Campari Girl' has generated free publicity for the brand as she became a celebrity.

Obviously, advertising was only one element in Campari's total marketing mix. It was a single strand in an integrated and well-planned marketing strategy for the brand. Other interacting factors certainly contributed to Campari's success. For example:

DISTRIBUTION GAINS

All outlet distribution rose from 48 per cent in 1975 to 58 per cent in 1979 with important gains in the grocery trade (Table 10.2).

Improved distribution between 1975 and 1976 helped accelerate Campari's growth, as the cut-back from 1976 to 1977 tended to check sales performance.

Over the period 1975–1979 distribution gains were definitely operating in Campari's favour. However, the extra sales generated were significantly greater than would have been expected from a 10 per cent improvement in distribution. Campari's increase in sales cannot be explained just by distribution gains.

TABLE 10.2: DISTRIBUTION OF CAMPARI

	All outlets	All on-licences	All off-licences	Specialists	Grocers
1975	48	51	37	69	18
1976	54	58	38	72	21
1977	51	55	39	71	25
1978	56	61	40	71	25
1979	58	61	45	75	32

Stats (MR).

PROMOTIONS

A series of imaginative and successful promotions, including 'Miss Campari' competitions tying in with the advertising campaign and special promotions for the trade and publicans, has been organized.

FREE PUBLICITY

Unlike many advertisers who graft famous stars onto their brands and borrow from their reputation or style, we created an exclusive Campari property in the form of Lorraine Chase. The brand has benefited enormously from free press coverage and television exposure as 'The Campari Girl' developed into a personality. The value of this free spin-off publicity is impossible to quantify.

OPTICS

The distribution of pub optics increased from 3 to 17 per cent between 1975 and 1980, and served to draw attention to Campari in this important public decision-making environment.

Nevertheless, we would argue that in 1976 the changes in Campari's advertising represented the single most influential new factor in the brand's marketing. Our contention is that the advertising, firstly, by choosing the right medium for our message and, secondly, by creating a relevant, vivid and memorable campaign, had the most dramatic effect on the 1976 sales off-take, and helped sustain growth thereafter.

The effectiveness of the advertising campaign for Campari can be demonstrated in two ways.

Sales

Regular Awareness and Usage checks showed healthy increases in both awareness and trial of Campari, which suggested that more people were learning about the brand and that we were succeeding in attracting new trialists (Table 10.3).

TABLE 10.3: CAMPARI AWARENESS AND TRIAL

	Pre		Post		
% *All adults*	1973	1975	1976	1977	1979
Aware	60	66	73	79	82
Tried	21	20	25	30	30

BMRB Access.

Encouragingly, the research also indicated that we were achieving the objective of attracting new, younger drinkers to the brand (Table 10.4).

TABLE 10.4: CAMPARI AGE PROFILE

	Pre	Post			
Tried Campari in last 3 months	1975	1976	1977	1978	1979
Age: 15–34	35	41	47	53	47
35–54	42	28	29	31	36
55+	22	30	23	15	16
Total	100	100	100	100	100

BMRB Access.

More significantly, Findlater Matta's ex-factory sales responded very sharply and immediately, and have continued to grow since (Figure 10.1).

Sales in any one year can be fairly erratic because of the artificial interference of the Budget, so it is more meaningful to look at growth over the entire advertised period. Campari's average annual sales have increased at the rate of 15.5 per cent.

This achievement cannot be attributed to general market trends. Campari has grown more quickly than total spirits, including whisky, gin and vermouth. Only vodka can rival Campari's performance over this period (Figure 10.2).

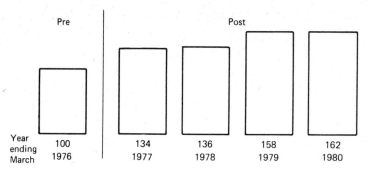

Figure 10.1. *Campari indexed ex-factory sales.*

The selection of television as the prime national medium throughout the campaign was an integral part of the brand's strategy for attracting a wider base of users. Television was clearly the right medium, and it greatly assisted Campari's buoyant sales. However, the staggering 34 per cent leap in Campari's case sales in the first year of the campaign cannot be due to the potency of the medium alone.

In 1976, the brand had by no means a heavyweight advertising presence. The 1975 and 1976 advertising budgets were virtually identical – £230 200 and £236 000 – without allowing for media inflation. The creative content of the advertising undoubtedly helped stretch a modest budget by stimulating people's imaginations.

Increased weight of advertising can be discounted as a factor in Campari's continued growth. Although Campari's advertising expenditure since 1976 has more or less kept pace with inflation, it has not increased significantly in real terms. The 1979 ITV strike meant an actual drop in Campari's advertising spend, and this was reflected in disappointing sales figures for the year.

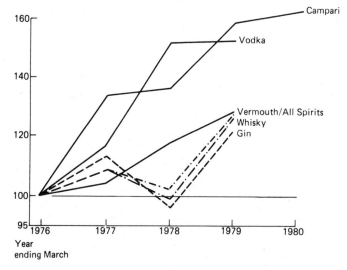

Figure 10.2. *Indexed sales: Campari versus other spirits.*

Consumer Behaviour

In the area of consumer behaviour, the contribution of the advertising content is undisputed. The campaign delivered a new and relevant suggestion about how to drink Campari. It was designed to make the drink more acceptable to a wider number of drinkers.

The regular Awareness and Usage monitor showed drinkers of Campari and lemonade rising steeply and the only possible source of the idea was the advertising (Table 10.5).

TABLE 10.5: HOW CAMPARI WAS DRUNK ON THE LAST OCCASION

	Pre	Post			
	1975	1976	1977	1978	1979
With soda	28	26	25	25	26
With lemonade	10	26	31	35	40
Neat	29	25	24	18	16

BMRB Access.

Moreover, the popularity of lemonade did not appear to disturb the Campari and soda drinker in the least. Thus we had met another key campaign objective.

That the effectiveness of Campari advertising can be measured in volume sales increases ahead of the total spirits market is impressive. That it is also reflected in such a striking behavioural shift is quite exceptional. The advertising not only transformed Campari literally into a different kind of drink, and one that appealed to a different type of person from the Campari and soda loyalist, but also succeeded in modifying people's drinking behaviour in a dramatic way. The advertising catapulted Campari into an era of growth in which new, younger trialists were attracted to the brand, and more people were encouraged to enjoy the drink.

11
Mini in 1979

INTRODUCTION

Leo Burnett were appointed by British Leyland in Autumn 1978 to handle advertising for the Mini. The detailed advertising brief was received in late November 1978, with a target airdate of 29th January 1979 for the television element of the new 1979 campaign.

This is an account of the development of that campaign, and an assessment of its effectiveness.

BUSINESS BACKGROUND

The British Leyland Mini is one of the great postwar success stories of the British car industry.

Mini was a revolutionary design when launched in 1959, and 20 years later it was still British Leyland's best-selling car – but in very different circumstances to those it had enjoyed in the 1960s.

In the 1960s Mini dominated the UK small-car market sector; for most purposes it was the sector. But in the early 1970s a new generation of small hatchbacks was launched. These vehicles were able to offer family motoring in a much more credible fashion than Mini could – they had more of the attributes of larger cars, most notably a family-sized luggage capacity (Mini's boot remains a standing joke even among its owners). They made the small car sector a fiercely competitive environment. Not only did Mini have to face demonstrably superior product claims in a number of aspects, it also had to cope with very high levels of competitive advertising expenditure and promotion.

Mini's volume sales and sector share history from 1973 to 1978 are shown in Table 11.1.

TABLE 11.1: MINI SALES AND SECTOR SHARE, 1973 TO 1978

Year	Sales ('000)	Share of small-car sector %
1973	96	49
1974	90	45
1975	85	44
1976	81	42
1977	60	28
1978	73	27

It is a picture of consistent decline (the volume recovery in 1978 reflects an industry sales trend, not a Mini revival).

Thus, the background to the 1979 Mini advertising task was of declining trends in both volume sales (1978 apart) and sector share. And the task has also to be judged in the context of the very real image difficulties facing British Leyland at the time. These difficulties were due in part to British Leyland's ageing car range: Mini was and is the oldest member of that range (and thus in a very real danger of being perceived as obsolete).

1979 VOLUME AND SHARE OBJECTIVES

The 1978 Mini sales results were 72 600 units: a 27 per cent share of the small car sector.

The 1979 Mini volume and share objectives laid down in the Marketing Plan were 78 600 units; a projected 28 per cent share of the small car sector, which required a reversal of the long-term trend.

THE 1979 ADVERTISING OBJECTIVE

Available consumer research on Mini showed the car to have all the ingredients of a 'classic' popular car:

1. It is a much-loved institution among the British motoring population: most drivers have driven a Mini; for many it was their first car.
2. People talk about their Mini with affection; they give them nicknames. Mini has a distinct personality.
3. That personality is bound up with Mini's traditional virtues. Mini remains a truly excellent town car – it is seen as economical, nippy, manoeuvrable, with excellent road-holding. And it's also cheeky, youthful and fun to drive.

But because people in the market for a small car no longer had to buy Mini, since they could now get a hatchback that would perform the family transport role more efficiently, by 1979 a lot of potential purchasers' memories of Mini were out of date. They remembered the drawstring door latches and the sliding side windows, both long replaced. And because they had an image of Mini as out of date, the car was no longer on the shopping list.

The 1979 advertising objective was quite simply to get the car back on the shopping list: to get potential customers into the showroom where they could see for themselves that 1979 Minis had been brought up to date without sacrificing the car's traditional virtues.

Three main ways of accomplishing the advertising task were identified:

(i) A theme campaign with the creative task of encapsulating Mini's brand personality in its traditional strengths.
(ii) The carrying through of the theme campaign to the point of sale in the showroom, and use in trade motivation and dealer support advertising.
(iii) Tactical campaigns capitalizing on 'special events' in 1979, notably Mini's 20th birthday, and the launch of limited editions.

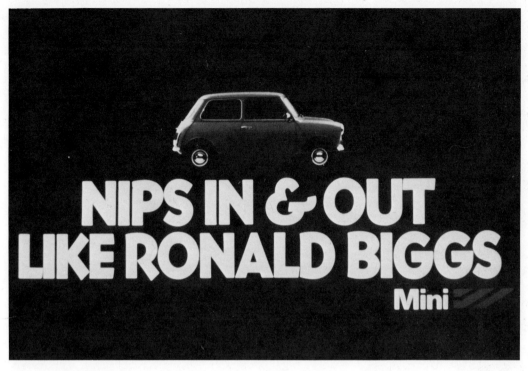

Mini press advertisement.

THEME CREATIVE STRATEGY AND EXECUTION

The essence of the theme creative strategy was to encapsulate Mini's brand personality in its traditional strengths of manoeuvrability and road-holding.

The consumer proposition was that Mini has the best manoeuvrability and road-holding of any small car, with support for this in its turning circle and acceleration, and in its centre of gravity and the qualities given by front wheel drive and the transverse engine.

And tonally the execution had to reflect the brand personality:

—fun
—cheekiness
—classlessness
—uniqueness ('you don't just drive a car, you drive a Mini')

The theme campaign used television, press and posters. There was a further creative constraint on the television execution: it had to be on air nine weeks after first briefing, and this interval included the Christmas holiday period.

The commercial devised within this constraint was unique among contemporary car advertising: it was nearly all in black and white and it was animated.

It opens on the word 'Mini', white out of a black background. The soundtrack begins with the sound of a driver's footsteps approaching a car, the driver getting into it, and the car starting up. As the car moves off, so does the dot above the first 'i' in the word Mini on the screen. A voice-over describes the manoeuvrability and road-holding of Mini, while the dot illustrates this by manoeuvring in, around and about the letters of the parent word. As the voice-over talks about the turning circle of the car the dot comes up outside the final letter 'i', circles its dot, and returns to its original position. The final frame shows a Mini in profile with the Austin Morris logo and the voice-over 'Nothing moves like a Mini'.

The voice-over reflects the car's personality not only in the script but also in the voices (there are two versions: Penelope Keith and Kenneth Williams).

Press and posters used the same execution: black background, white headline, profile colour shot of Mini, Austin Morris logo. The personality and the proposition were summed up in the headlines:

'Nips in and out like Ronald Biggs'
'More gripping than Agatha Christie'
'A tighter lock than Mick McManus'
'Better in jams than strawberries'
'Gets around town like Casanova'

Also, in two executions for the more specialist male-interest magazines:

'Gets out of more tight spots than Flash Gordon'
'Does a better turn than Fiona Richmond'

The 'Ronald Biggs' execution generated considerable editorial publicity (estimated as equivalent to advertising space worth in excess of £100 000).

All the poster executions were translated into showroom posters and banners for use at point of sale.

TACTICAL ADVERTISING

Tactical press advertising was devised to capitalize on specific events in 1979. The objective was to use these events to generate further consumer interest in Mini, again essentially to get the car on the shopping list, and to get potential customers into the showroom to reappraise Mini.

For example:

—for the launch of the Mini Special: 'You take the Daimler, dear, I'll take the Mini'.
—for Mini's 20th Birthday: 'After 20 years we think we may be onto something good'.
—for the British Saloon Car Championship: 'Meet the last 2 British Saloon Car Champions'.
—for the Mini Rally Championship: 'Are you interested in a dirty weekend?'.

THE 1979 MEDIA BUDGET

The media budget available for 1979 was smaller than that for either of the previous two years (excluding poster expenditure, which represents Mini's share of the British Leyland poster holding and is roughly constant in real terms year on year) (Table 11.2).

Thus the task had to be accomplished on a reduced budget.

TABLE 11.2: MEDIA BUDGET, 1977 TO 1979

	£'000 (*excluding posters*)
1977	808
1978	679
1979	566

MEDIA STRATEGY

The target audience for the campaign was, and remains, prospective buyers of small cars. In particular, it is those prospective buyers whose needs are more appropriate to the sort of personal transport offered by Mini, as opposed to the family transport offered by a small hatchback.

They are likely to be, if buying the sole car in the household:

—younger
—single, or married without children
—unisex
—urban

Or they could be buying the second car in the household.

Media choice was:

1. Television: despite the bias of the target audience towards light viewers, television gave reasonable cover; the presence of television is a considerable dealer motivator; and, above all, it offered great creative opportunity.
2. Posters: to extend coverage and frequency, especially among light viewers.
3. Specialist press (male and motoring): to increase coverage of men.
4. Monochrome press: for the dealer support programme.

CAMPAIGN EVALUATION

The quantitative criterion for the evaluation of the 1979 campaign is sales (evaluation of subsequent campaigns will be greatly assisted by British Leyland's newly inaugurated Advertising Tracking System, but these data came onstream for the first time in February 1980).

The 1979 campaign was totally directed at getting Mini onto prospective buyers' shopping lists and getting the prospects into the showroom, and there were no other obvious factors which in 1979 exerted abnormal influence on the customer (either positive or negative):

(i) The dealer network was reasonably stable, hence no problems in distribution.
(ii) There was no abnormal promotional activity (such as a cut-price campaign).
(iii) There was no product change to alter the basic consumer perception of the car.
(iv) There was no major competitive launch in the small-car sector.
(v) There was no major corporate activity (such as the British Leyland 'Buy British' Campaign of early 1980).

TABLE 11.3: MINI SALES AND SECTOR SHARE, 1978 AND 1979

	Sales	Share of small-car sector %
1978	72 619	27.4
1979 Target	78 560	28.6
1979 Achievement	82 938	30.2

The sales results indicate a resounding success: volume sales are the highest since 1975, the sector share trend is reversed, and the targets set in 1978 are comfortably beaten (Table 11.3).

A volume sales increase of 14 per cent was achieved with an advertising budget reduced in sterling terms by 17 per cent.

Qualitative criteria also show success:

—The executions attracted favourable editorial publicity (notably the Ronald Biggs poster).
—The campaign was judged a considerable motivating influence with the dealer network.
—And in 1980 it has proved its quality as a long-term campaign, both in television, to stress product development (the 'Quiet Mini' execution to demonstrate the new sound-proofing package), and in print, to stress economy ('It will give you a run for Yamani').

CONCLUSION

The 1979 advertising campaign for Mini was very effective.

In a year where there were no major changes in other elements of the marketing environment for Mini, apart from the advertising campaign, a major sales increase was achieved. And this increase was achieved on a reduced advertising budget.

The success of the campaign was due to a single-minded creative approach which concentrated on Mini's great and traditional strengths, strengths which remained the reason why the car was as relevant to consumer needs in 1979 as it was in 1959.

By concentrating on these strengths in executions which reflected the positive aspects of Mini's personality, the campaign achieved its objective of putting Mini truly back on the shopping list.

And it rammed this home by ruthlessly pursuing the objective not only in consumer advertising but also in the showroom, in dealer motivation, and in all other available aspects of the selling mix. It was conceived, and it worked, as a campaign utilizing and integrating all relevant means of exposure.

12

The Effect of Advertising on Sanatogen Multivitamins

INTRODUCTION

This chapter reviews the past sales performance of the Sanatogen Vitamin brand and the effect that advertising has had on its recent sales increases.

BACKGROUND

Sanatogen was originally a nerve tonic which Fisons Limited acquired in the thirties.

In 1963 the company launched a range of multivitamin products under the Sanatogen name with an aggressive advertising programme. Within two years Sanatogen Multivitamins had achieved market leadership.

The brand grew steadily until 1974 when factory sales, both in sterling and unit terms, slumped drastically (Table 12.1).

TABLE 12.1: EX-FACTORY SALES, 1970 TO 1975

Indices	1970	1971	1972	1973	1974	1975
Sterling ('000)	100	103	117	153	124	127
Units (packs 000)	100	101	113	114	90	81

Consumer purchase data from Nielsen generally showed trends parallel to the ex-factory data. Differences were due to the fact that Nielsen does not audit Boots. Nielsen also indicated that the market outside Boots was sliding even more precipitously than was Sanatogen (Table 12.2).

TABLE 12.2: NIELSEN UNITS, 1970 TO 1975

Indices	1970	1971	1972	1973	1974	1975
Market	100	96	100	100	90	85
Sanatogen	100	111	124	125	113	109

THE DIAGNOSIS

McCormick's were appointed advertising agents for Sanatogen and all the products of the Pharmaceutical Division of Fisons in 1975.

After extensive study of the available data and conducting consumer research, the following facts emerged:

1. Sanatogen as a brand name was seen as old fashioned and dated. It was respected for its traditional values, but a majority of people thought of it as a tonic – or, even more often, a tonic wine – not a vitamin range.
2. Usership of vitamins in general was low and declining and they were of low interest value amongst non-users.
3. Users saw vitamins as a quasi-medicinal product to correct a sub-par feeling, not as a means of safeguarding good health.
4. The market depended on Sanatogen for its leadership and promotion.
5. The vitamin manufacturers (including Sanatogen) believed vitamins were winter orientated, while those consumers who used vitamins took them all year round.

The overall marketing objectives were then set:

1. Arrest the brand's sales decline and rebuild its consumer franchise.
2. Expand the total market for vitamins while maintaining and growing Sanatogen's leadership of it.

BRAND OBJECTIVE ONE

The Media

This had previously been national press. It was changed to women's press, which provided:

1. A way to focus advertising spending on the people who research had identified not only as prime purchasers but also as major users.
2. Colour, to liven up the brand's grey, dated image.
3. A sympathetic reading environment.

The spend pattern was also modified to even out the previous bias towards the winter months, and therefore reflect consumer purchasing habits, as well as provide a more consistent spread of advertising messages.

The Message

Historically, Sanatogen had used a typically proprietary medicine advertising theme, promising to provide tired, middle-aged people with longer, healthier, more active lives. This appeared at odds with the attitudes of vitamin users and non-users alike, and, we believed, was contributing to the geriatric image of the product.

A new creative strategy was devised to:

1. Establish the use of vitamins as an aid to healthy living for normal people.

2. Present credible reasons for taking vitamins.
3. Present Sanatogen as an up-to-date product, totally attuned to today's lifestyle.
4. Establish the use of Sanatogen vitamins as an everyday habit as natural as brushing your teeth.

The creative technique used was to identify people whose photographs seemed to convey a feeling of health, well-being and quiet happiness to a cross-section of women.

These photographs formed 'The Sanatogen Smile' campaign. Body copy presented a reasoned, non-strident, very credible case for the daily use of vitamins as a kind of health insurance policy.

The Results

The recovery of the brand was quite rapid, and within 20 months it had returned to its 1970 level of unit sales (Table 12.3).

The decline of the total market had been arrested, whilst Sanatogen began to grow again (Table 12.4).

TABLE 12.3: EX-FACTORY SALES, 1970 TO 1977

						'Sanatogen Smile'	
Indices	1970	1972	1973	1974	1975	1976	1977
Sterling (£'000)	100	117	153	124	127	158	197
Units (packs 000)	100	113	114	90	81	88	100

TABLE 12.4: NIELSEN UNITS, 1970 TO 1977

						'Sanatogen Smile'	
Indices	1970	1972	1973	1974	1975	1976	1977
Market	100	100	100	90	85	78	78
Sanatogen	100	124	125	113	109	111	120

BRAND OBJECTIVE TWO

With the brand's ex-factory unit sales back to its previous position, the way was now clear to pursue Objective Two – to build the market and increase Sanatogen's sales and develop its market position with it. A price increase during 1977 provided the additional funds to do this.

The Media

Television offered the brand:

(a) A medium never used before by any adult multivitamin product, and
(b) The ability to mount an area test and monitor its effectiveness in producing sales.

Stills from Sanatogen Multivitamins television advertisement.

All through life, your
body changes.

But sometimes it changes more quickly.

That's when there may be a chance of vitamin
deficiency. And that's when Sanatogen Vitamins
can help.

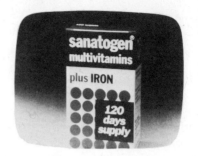

They contain essential vitamins and minerals, to help ensure good health.

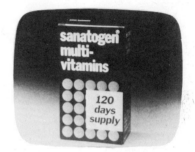

So, whether you're growing up, pregnant, or at retirement age, Sanatogen vitamins help you stay on top of the changes in your life.

**Sanatogen Vitamins.
One a day, every day.**

A test was implemented in London and Southern over the eight-week, September/October Nielsen period in 1978, at a national equivalent of £250 000.

The Message

Creatively, it would have been ideal to extend 'The Sanatogen Smile' story to television, but the strict regulations set by the IBA did not permit this. The IBA states that only three categories of people could be in need of vitamin supplementation: growing children, pregnant/lactating mothers, and the elderly. This apparent problem was turned into an opportunity. A script based on these categories was prepared, approved and produced with the only restriction that it could not be shown before 9 pm.

The Results

Nielsen sterling data were used to monitor the test (unit data by area were not available) (Table 12.5).

TABLE 12.5: NIELSEN UNITS, 1977 VS. 1978

Area	Consumer sales Sept/Oct 1978 vs. 1977	Brand shares % 1977	1978
TV test area (London & Southern)			
Total market	+38%	100	100
Sanatogen	+70%	35	43
Control area (remainder UK)			
Total market	+16%	100	100
Sanatogen	+16%	37	37

This indication that television, overlaid on the Sanatogen Smile campaign in women's press, could produce up to a fifty per cent increase in consumer purchases of Sanatogen (and pull the market up with it) was immensely encouraging, since any increase of this magnitude, if sustained for only four months, would generate enough incremental gross profit to recover the cost of the incremental advertising.

To confirm the indications, test activity was extended to a larger area for the four-month period January to April 1979. Spending was again at a national equivalent of £250 000.

Nielsen sterling data were again used as a measurement device (Table 12.6).

TABLE 12.6: NIELSEN UNITS, 1978 VS. 1979

Area	Consumer sales Jan/April 1979 vs. 1978	Brand shares % 1978	1979
TV test area (London, Southern, ATV & Harlech)			
Total market	+31%	100	100
Sanatogen	+66%	33	42
Control area (remainder UK)			
Total market	+15%	100	100
Sanatogen	+13%	38	37

With incremental sales in excess of 50 per cent, we confirmed that, for a four-month period, the commerical viability of television and women's press was proven. Extra funds were therefore requested and provided by Fisons to permit the use of TV advertising nationally, in late 1979.

At the end of 1979, the Sanatogen Multivitamin position was as shown in Tables 12.7 to 12.9.

TABLE 12.7: EX-FACTORY SALES, 1970 TO 1979

| Indices | 1970 | 1974 | 'Sanatogen Smile' | | Television and 'Sanatogen Smile' | |
			1976	1977	1978	1979
Sterling (£'000)	100	124	158	197	286	429
Units (packs 000)	100	90	88	100	141	201

TABLE 12.8: CONSUMER PURCHASES (NIELSEN UNITS)

Indices	1970	1974	1977	1978	1979
Total market	100	90	78	96	100
Sanatogen	100	113	120	150	186

TABLE 12.9: BRAND SHARE (NIELSEN STERLING)

Brand	1970	1974	1977	1978	1979
Sanatogen	29	34	36	38	42
Haliborange	28	24	19	20	18
Superplenamins	9	9	7	5	5
Vykmin	8	10	11	11	11
All others	26	23	27	26	24
Total	100	100	100	100	100

Nielsen does not audit Boots and therefore cannot measure sales of that company's own brands of vitamins, which have always led the market in penetration (but probably not in value). However, the Sanatogen advertising campaign has helped Sanatogen narrow Boots' lead significantly, as TGI indicates (Table 12.10).

TABLE 12.10: TGI UNITS

Brand usage	1976	1977	1978	1979
Boots	27.5	30.1	27.2	26.8
Sanatogen	16.6	18.1	20.0	21.6

ADVERTISING SPEND

Whilst the advertising spend has grown substantially, the A/S ratio has declined significantly (Table 12.11).

TABLE 12.11: ADVERTISING SPEND

£'000	1972	1974	1977	1978	1979
Index	100	131	175	280	313
A/S Ratio	29	36	30	33	25

CONSUMER USERSHIP

In addition to improving Sanatogen's sales, share and profitability, the advertising campaign (Sanatogen spends over 60 per cent of all advertising on vitamins) appears to be making significant changes in consumer usage of vitamins.

As noted previously, 1974–75 vitamin usership was in decline, Sanatogen's penetration was slowly being eroded, and its profile was skewed to the older consumer than the market as a whole.

TGI data now show:

(i) a reversal in total usership and an increase in Sanatogen's penetration (Table 12.12), and
(ii) its age profile becoming younger (Table 12.13).

TABLE 12.12: TGI DATA

Usership/Penetration (%)	1971	1975	1977	1978	1979
Total usership	21.9	18.6	16.4	20.3	20.7
Sanatogen penetration	3.5	3.3	3.0	4.1	4.5

TABLE 12.13: TGI DATA

Age profiles	1971 T	1971 S	1975 T	1975 2S	1977 T	1977 S	1978 T	1978 S	1979 T	1979 S
15–34	31.5	23.8	33.8	27.8	34.1	30.7	35.7	31.0	38.4	35.8
35–44	16.9	17.7	17.2	18.0	16.7	14.9	16.5	17.5	15.5	16.3
45+	51.6	58.4	48.9	54.3	49.2	54.5	47.7	51.5	46.3	47.9

Key: T = total market; S = Sanatogen. All figures are percentages.

CONCLUSION

The evidence presented shows how the effective use of advertising has improved the sales performance of Sanatogen Multivitamins over the two two-year periods set (see Figures 12.1 and 12.2).

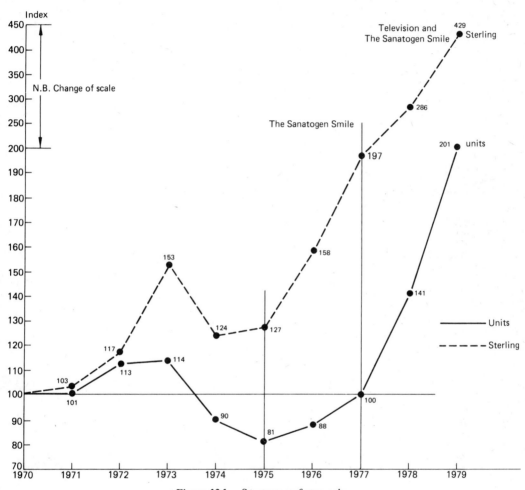

Figure 12.1. *Sanatogen ex-factory sales.*

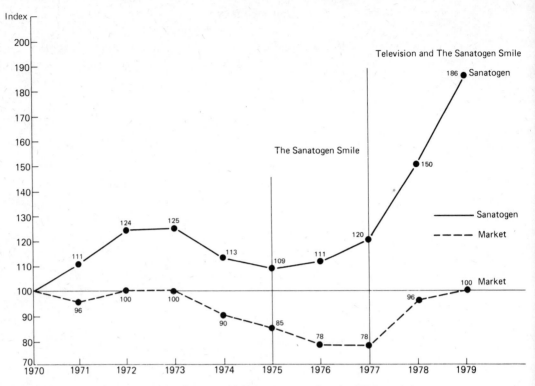

Figure 12.2.   *Sanatogen Multivitamins vs. total market (Nielsen units).*

13
Pretty Polly

INTRODUCTION

Pretty Polly was founded in 1920 in Sutton in Ashfield, Nottinghamshire, as a producer of ladies' silk, rayon and lisle stockings. By 1939 the company was soundly established with a reputation for quality and a brand name that, if not one of the prewar leaders like Bear Brand, Kayser or Aristoc, was, nonetheless, well respected.

Resuming after the war, production switched to nylon in 1946–47 and by 1959, when the company became a wholly owned subsidiary of Thomas Tilling Limited, Pretty Polly was producing 5000 dozens per week.

With the retirement of the original management in 1960, Pretty Polly embarked on an expansion programme that progressively took the company to a weekly output of 240 000 dozen in 1974 and from a market share of less than 5 per cent in 1960 to over 20 per cent of a much larger market in 1974. By 1975, Pretty Polly was the largest individual producer in the UK, among the six largest in the world, and had, under the Pretty Polly logo, brand leadership in the UK.

BUSINESS BACKGROUND

In assessing the advertising strategy of Pretty Polly and the effect of that advertising on its progress, it is essential to review the background to the ladies' hosiery industry against which the company had to operate in the crisis year of 1974–75. In 1973 and 1974, the UK hosiery industry was faced with very severe problems, most of which were common throughout the developed world.

1. Worldwide overcapacity to the order of 30 to 40 per cent.
2. The prospect of a positive decline in market off-take due to the emergence of casual attire, epitomized by the jeans explosion with women's legs being increasingly covered up.
3. An excessively fragmented industry, few of whose members were earning a profit at all and many of whom were on the verge of liquidation.
4. An emerging trend of expanding sales through supermarkets with the threat of even more savage price competition if the product were treated as a loss leader unbranded commodity. The weak state of the industry could easily be exploited by the powerful retail groups to ensure unprofitable selling prices ex the manufacturer.

5. A retail structure which encouraged a dominance of 'own label' or unbranded products. Recognized national brands accounted for less than 14 per cent of the entire market.

6. A very serious threat of import penetration from the low cost Italian industry, which had already begun to dominate the other major EEC markets (Germany, France and the Netherlands).

Early in 1974 Pretty Polly, which had, by that time, emerged as the leading national brand name with an overall market share of some 20 per cent in all categories (branded and unbranded), formulated a five-year plan. While recognizing the unfavourable immediate prospects, the plan was designed to create, by a coherent marketing strategy, a strong national brand position in the growth areas of the market. By so doing, the plan would enable Pretty Polly to control its own destiny rather than be essentially a faceless producer for major distribution outlets whose ability to switch purchases to the cheapest resources, i.e. Italy, would be encouraged by the establishment of an own label/unbranded commodity type market.

Success for Pretty Polly would require the company, whilst expanding its overall volume to 25 per cent of the home market, to increase the percentage of its sales that were made under the company's own brand name from 17 to 60 per cent by 1979 with an eventual target of 80 per cent by 1983.

The two vital areas of development would be:

1. Strengthening still further the existing conventional 'upmarket' branded sector sold through department stores and drapers. This sector was unlikely to grow in volume due to price pressure from the emerging supermarket sector but would still be crucial in maintaining a prestige image with the general public. With approximately 25 per cent of the overall market in this sector, it was vital for Pretty Polly, who was the leading brand in volume sales, to maintain their leadership and expand it by product innovation and exciting visual advertising. Success in this area would greatly assist our efforts to upgrade the emerging potential of the grocery sector.

2. The rapidly expanding grocery sector, embracing multiple grocers, co-operatives, symbol groups, cash'n carries and independent outlets, whose interest in the ladies' hosiery market was enhanced by the realization that this product field promised high volume sales. The enormous weekly traffic flow of women and the traditionally high drapery profit 'on returns' of 35 per cent, as compared with a 16 per cent rate or less for food items, would enable grocers to undercut the conventional drapery market and still enjoy above-average profits, should they operate on, for example, a 24 per cent margin.

Clearly it would be difficult to persuade the aggressive grocery sector to forgo its normal attitude of buying in the cheapest market an own label product and rely on outstanding value to create the volume sales they wished to attain. Equally, it could be dangerous to supply such outlets with a national brand range that would be subject to large scale price cutting and consequent loss of confidence in the prestige sector of the department stores and drapers.

That a solution to this problem was crucial is borne out by the fact that, between 1973 and 1979, drapers and department stores declined from 26 per cent of the total UK volume sales to 23 per cent: grocers and supermarkets expanded their share from 24 per cent of the total UK volume sales to 33 per cent and are still growing.

Pretty Polly press advertisements.

In order to avoid the apparent pitfalls, Pretty Polly set up a grocery range under the 'Galaxy by Pretty Polly' label with a more limited selection than in the drapery range. Confidence was preserved in the drapery sector by not utilizing the main Pretty Polly brand or including the higher fashion styles in the grocery range.

Similarly, the use of the Pretty Polly logo, in conjunction with the Galaxy brand name, was sufficient to encourage grocery consumers to purchase our product range, demonstrating to grocers that their retail customers did not necessarily want to buy the cheapest hosiery but welcomed the endorsement of a recognized hosiery name.

CORPORATE STRATEGY

Our objective of branded growth made a change in our distribution strategy essential. This involved a gradual withdrawal from two static and declining sectors of the market, namely, the conventional chain stores (Marks and Spencer, Littlewoods, British Home Stores, etc.) and the wholesale trade. These areas, in our opinion, had gone ex-growth and in any event would do nothing to enhance our 'branded' ambitions as they were wedded to own label activities.

In view of the necessity to advance on two fronts, both in the drapery sector and in grocery, we determined to operate a strong corporate strategy to strengthen further the franchise of the Pretty Polly name and to facilitate the move to increasing the volume of goods selling under the Pretty Polly logo in both sectors.

In order to achieve this, in addition to carrying the two floral 'Ps', already well recognized by consumers, throughout all our activities, we used the theme 'Pretty Polly Brings Back Lovely Legs'. This theme was highly appropriate in view of the fashion move toward casual attire, specifically jeans and trousers, and was used throughout, not only in all media, but also on point-of-sale material. Further utilization of this has been made in public relations activities, e.g. 'Lovely Legs' Fashion Shows, 'Lovely Legs' Competitions, etc. The aim was to achieve overall corporate synergy with activities on both fronts working to mutual advantage.

This submission is essentially the history of a campaign to expand the recognition of a brand name (mainly through advertising) in order to capture in a short period a dominant position in a rapidly developing new market sector, namely grocery. That this was achieved so completely and so profitably with a relatively modest expenditure is, in my opinion, a triumph for creative advertising. Other factors, such as manufacturing competence, the good fortune to assess correctly the market opportunities, and the ability to distribute were all vital, but, beyond all, lay the need for wide recognition of the Pretty Polly brand name.

CORPORATE MARKETING AND ADVERTISING OBJECTIVES 1975-1979

The objectives we were required to achieve, and against which our advertising strategy would be measured, were fairly clear:

1. Increase Pretty Polly brand awareness.
2. Increase our share of the prestige branded sales in the drapery sector.
3. Beneath the umbrella of increased brand awareness and increasing leadership in the

prestige branded sector, capture a dominant leadership position in the growing grocery sector under the Pretty Polly logo.

4. Improve profits.
5. Substantially increase the proportion of our total output marketed under the Pretty Polly logo label.
6. Contain import penetration.
7. Sustain our production capacity.
8. From increased profits, continue to invest heavily in the latest equipment, thereby ensuring the long-term viability of the business.

THE ADVERTISING CAMPAIGN AND STRATEGY

The campaign was essentially a medium-term one, over a five-year period, and whilst minor diversions were made in promoting one or two specific products, the theme throughout was a corporate image creating effort, built around the message 'Pretty Polly brings back lovely legs' and the general desirability of 'Legs *vs.* Jeans'.

For the purposes of this submission, it is appreciated that only advertisements appearing between June 1977 and June 1980 are significant, but our campaign started before then and still continues today.

Two articles on Pretty Polly's five-year strategy appeared in the leading trade journal of the industry, *Knitting International*, in April 1977 (midway through the campaign) and in November 1979, when its objectives had been achieved.

The major thrust was to be behind the main Pretty Polly name and a smaller campaign was created, parallel to it, in support of the specific range of hosiery we wished to market in the grocery sector.

Our advertising strategy was to utilize high-impact media to create a continuous prestige presence for the Pretty Polly name. This was essential to maintain and strengthen our position in the traditional drapery sector and to provide us with an umbrella of branded strength to assist our penetration of the grocery sector. Primary media from 1977 have been posters and magazines, as our product lends itself to dramatic visual imagery. Both 16-sheet London Underground and 48-sheet outdoor posters have been used.

The 16-sheet LTA posters have been used continuously and were selected because they afforded a threefold benefit:

1. They offer exposure to a high volume of women who tend to be more fashion conscious than elsewhere in the UK. It is estimated that 1.15 million women utilize the stations selected each month, and it is assessed that 4.5 million women will have the opportunity to see a Pretty Polly advertisement each year.
2. They gain exposure to key Head Office retail buyers, most of whom are based in London.
3. They gain exposure to major trade and consumer fashion editors – also based in London.

48-sheet outdoor PCSs have been used on average twice a year. They have been utilized in conjunction with magazine activity to give drama and importance to the Pretty Polly campaign. Although it is difficult to evaluate in true media terms the coverage achieved by posters, it is estimated that a PSC in one month would be seen 18 times by 80 per cent of ABC1 women aged 25 to 45.

The outdoor poster campaigns are timed to Spring and Autumn – the times of the year when hosiery benefits most from activity.

In conjunction with posters we have used both double and single colour pages in women's magazines. These provide additional frequency of exposure to our target audience and are able to explain product benefits in greater detail, as this is a more suitable medium to carry a fuller message. For campaign establishment, double pages are utilized, and thereafter single pages to obtain maximum frequency.

Within the umbrella of corporate coverage via magazines and posters, commercial radio has been utilized in support of 'Galaxy by Pretty Polly', our grocery range. Radio has been used for a number of reasons:

1. In 1977 radio was a very cost-effective medium for gaining coverage.
2. The requirement was to create awareness that a Pretty Polly brand was then available through supermarkets, rather than selling a purely glamour image. (Pretty Polly's glamour is established through the main media of posters and magazines.)
3. It is a highly flexible medium offering the facility of hitting consumers at prime shopping times.

The radio campaign bursts run over two alternate weeks delivering 40 per cent coverage of ILR women per week with an OTH of 5.5.

Wherever appropriate, throughout our marketing activities the corporate theme 'Pretty Polly brings back lovely legs' was utilized both in direct advertising and in supporting 'in-store' promotional activity.

Public relations activities also provided 'spin-off' for the corporate theme and considerable exposure for Pretty Polly in the form of fashion shows, the enormously successful Pretty Polly Miss Lovely Legs of Great Britain Competitions at the holiday camps and, finally, sponsorship of two major national events for women, namely, the British Ladies' Open Golf and the British Women's Open Squash Championships.

THE CREATIVE EFFORT IN ADVERTISING

A series of eye-catching, elegant posters and advertisements were created:

1975	'When was the last time …?' (Design Council Award 1975. Featured in One Hundred Great Advertisements.)
1976	'We don't do nasty things' (Design Council Award 1976)
June 1977	'Non-stop'
1978	'Under control'
1978	'Looks like jeans' (Gold Award – Institute of Marketing)
1979	'For girls who don't – Sheer extravagance' (Gold Award – Institute of Marketing 1979)
May 1980	'When was the last time …?' (Irish version) (A sensational debut in Ireland causing exceptional press comment.)

Several 30-second radio programmes were created for Galaxy in 1977, 1978 and 1979, among which the 1978 campaign was awarded a Silver Award (first in category) in the BBA Commercial Radio Awards.

ATTAINMENT OF OBJECTIVES

Whilst it is obvious the attainment of specific objectives cannot be attributed wholly to the effectiveness of advertising, equally it is perverse not to give it the benefit of its full share of the credit if objectives are attained, especially when the advertising has won awards from its own profession.

Objective 1: Increase in Pretty Polly Brand Awareness

See Table 13.1.

TABLE 13.1: PRETTY POLLY BRAND AWARENESS

	Spring 1976 %	Spring 1980 %	Change
Pretty Polly	43	55	+12
Marks and Spencer	52	44	−8
Bear Brand	47	35	−12
Kayser	26	22	−4
Aristoc	26	27	+1
British Home Stores	21	20	−1
Littlewoods	21	21	N/C

NOP, March 1980.

Objective 2: Increase in Share of Prestige Branded Sales in Drapery Sector

Despite a 20 per cent decline in volume in this sector between 1974 and 1979, Pretty Polly volume held steady and its share of the reduced market increased significantly (Table 13.2).

Within the overall total, the ratio of the high-profit items improved very sharply and, with it, profitability (see Objective 4).

TABLE 13.2: BRAND SHARE IN DRAPERY SECTION

Year	Branded sales (million dozen)	Share of sector %
1975	1.35	25
1976	1.38	28
1977	1.29	32
1978	1.33	34
1979	1.32	34

Objective 3: Establish Leadership Under a Pretty Polly Logo Brand in the Rapidly Growing Grocery Sector

Perhaps the greatest individual achievement of the five-year strategy has been the significant leadership attained by Galaxy by Pretty Polly in a market sector that now is the largest single market segment, at 33 per cent, and one that is still growing and should reach 45 per cent by 1984. Galaxy at 21 per cent is three times larger than the nearest single brand (Table 13.3) and still growing.

TABLE 13.3: BRAND SHARE OF GROCERY MARKET

Brand	August 1976 %	December 1979 %	Change
Galaxy by Pretty Polly	9	20.6	+11.6
Bear Brand	5.2	6.1	+1
Nikki by Pretty Polly	NIL	4	+4
Kayser	1	3.7	+2.7
Sainsbury own label	N/A	7.5 ⎫	Estimated to
Tesco own label	N/A	6.5 ⎬	be only
Co-op own label	N/A	6.5 ⎭	marginally bigger than 1976 as % share

Nielsen, January 1980. (No data available prior to August 1976.)

Objective 4: Improve Our Profits

As a result of selling more of our products under our own brand and improving the product mix ratio, our profits have recovered sharply in the three years 1977–1979 to successive new records from the extreme problems of 1976. An increase of over 100 per cent in each of the three years 1977/1978/1979 from the previous figure is a reasonable achievement, particularly in textiles. The return on funds must be considered satisfactory as an average and the pay-back on the advertising and marketing investment over the period (absorbed in the operating costs) is obviously acceptable (Table 13.4).

TABLE 13.4: PROFITS

	1976	1977	1978	1979
Net profit (£'000)	281	927	1857	4036
Return on funds (%)	3.1	11.5	22.7	43.0

Objective 5: Increase in Share of the Company's Total Sales Under the Pretty Polly Logo (Table 13.5)

The eventual aim must be to achieve approximately 80 per cent, leaving the balance for specialized own label supplied in conjunction with our Pretty Polly labels. The present figure of 60 per cent compares with a figure of 17 per cent of our total production in Pretty Polly labels in 1973.

TABLE 13.5

	1973	1977	1978	1979
% of sales in Pretty Polly logo	17	39	50	60

Objective 6: Contain Import Penetration

The serious level of penetration by the low cost Italian Stocking Industry into the key hosiery markets of Europe by 1975 (Table 13.6) had caused a most alarming collapse in local production capabilities. The strength of the two leading British companies, Pretty Polly and Courtaulds had, by their competitive pricing and modern facilities, kept Italy out, but only at the expense of exceptionally low profits in 1975–76. By increasing the strength of the Pretty Polly brand in the grocery sector, the likelihood of retailers switching to imports has been reduced. By the end of 1979 over 90 per cent of tights and stockings sold in the UK are being made by British firms, whereas UK textiles, in general, average nearer 50 per cent of imports, and some categories are over 70 per cent imported.

TABLE 13.6: PERCENTAGE IMPORT PENETRATION IN MAJOR EUROPEAN MARKETS OF LADIES' HOSIERY (MAINLY FROM ITALY, ISRAEL AND EAST GERMANY)

Country	1976	1979
UK	7	9
Germany	30	50
Benelux	55	70
France	25	30

Objectives 7 and 8: Earn Sufficient Profits to Sustain Our Production Capabilities and Invest in New Equipment

Our overall capacity at some 240 000 dozen per week is identical to that in 1974. It is, however, made on even more up-to-date equipment and with 20 per cent fewer employees. Productivity has increased rapidly for the last four years.

Investment at a very high rate has taken place right through the profit decline of 1975 and 1976, with over £7 million invested in machinery, building and working capital between 1975 and 1979.

All this has been provided from retained profits and depreciation after paying reasonable dividends to our shareholders.

CONCLUSIONS

As the Chief Executive of Pretty Polly since 1961 I have been involved in monitoring every major advertising campaign created for the company since that time. By the criteria that matter, namely, expanding sales and increasing profits, I am totally convinced our advertising funds have more than justified their expenditure and are effective. The figures prove it.

Over the period of Spring 1977 to Spring 1980 that is covered by the terms of the IPA Competition, the direct advertising costs were £1 250 000. After paying for the advertising incurred, the extra trading profit earned over and above the trading profit earned in the equivalent three-year period 1974–1976 was £4 800 000. Not all of this is due to advertising but good advertising was a key factor and deserves its share of the credit.

In formulating the five-year advertising plan, full use was made of attitude surveys covering the company, its packaging and its products. The basic grocery concept was test marketed in Scotland and the North East for 18 months between 1973 and 1975, achieving exceptional penetration and acceptance. Full national coverage was then initiated.

Monitoring results was crucial and Pretty Polly was, and still is, to my knowledge, the only hosiery company to have a full two-monthly retail audit from Nielsen on hosiery sales in grocery. Backed up by twice-yearly NOP surveys on brand awareness, an accurate picture of progress by area and retail outlet has been achieved. Results of our principal competitors are included in our Nielsen survey in order to measure their strengths and weaknesses relative to ourselves.

An Above the Line Advertising Budget limited to less than 3 per cent of turnover (a modest figure for fashion goods in the branded sector) has called for exceptional qualities of effective advertising from our agency - luckily we have received it.

I would not normally detail the direct sales from any particular advertisement featuring a specific product as I feel it is hard to separate the merit of the product from that of the advertising over a short period. In fact, the three advertisements that were so particularized between 1977 and 1979 all resulted in exceptional sales, relative to our expectations, and I have detailed their performance in Table 13.7.

TABLE 13.7: DIRECT REACTION IN SALES AND PROFITS TO SPECIFIC ADVERTISEMENTS 1977-1980

A. Non-stop
Total cost of campaigns in 1977 and 1978 = £255 000

Additional sales over 1976 level:
1977 = 143 000 dozen, yielding £187 000 profit
1978 = 266 000 dozen, yielding £464 000 profit
1979 = 256 000 dozen, yielding £581 000 profit

The construction now represents over 35 per cent of the entire UK sales of support-type hosiery.

B. Under Control (new product)
Total cost of campaigns in 1978 and 1979 = £127 000

1978 sales = 14 000 dozen, yielding profit of £31 000
1979 sales = 68 000 dozen, yielding profit of £155 000

Garment now established as best-selling product in category.

C. Sheer Extravagance (new product)
Combining a corporate 'anti-jeans' theme and our most prestigious Sheer tight, the advertisement helped create a demand we only now, after 14 months, are able to meet.

Total cost of campaigns in 1979   = £175 000
Profit from sales over period   = £210 000
Plus benefit of corporate exposure and prestige from Gold Award in 1979.

In addition, I have detailed the progress of a special corporate campaign in Spring (1980) in the Republic of Ireland as, in this single instance, we are able to measure advertising impact in an isolated market, hitherto unstimulated by advertising. An advertising investment of £130 000 is likely to yield £200 000 extra profit in less than 12 months (see the appendix at the end of this chapter).

However successful these individual cases were, they are still only incidental to the major value of our long-term creative advertisements in support of the brand name strategy. Pretty

Polly has been the most consistent advertiser in the British hosiery industry over the past 19 years and perhaps it is no coincidence that we are also probably the only major company that has averaged a return of over 17 per cent on its funds over a period of exceptional competition and difficulty.

Finally one figure may be of interest in illustrating how consistent advertising and expanding sales usually result in better value and keener prices relative to the Retail Price Index (Figure 13.1). Obviously, modern facilities and manufacturing competence are relevant factors, but the confidence and sales élan engendered by successful advertising encourage capital investment and high productivity. It certainly is the case with Pretty Polly.

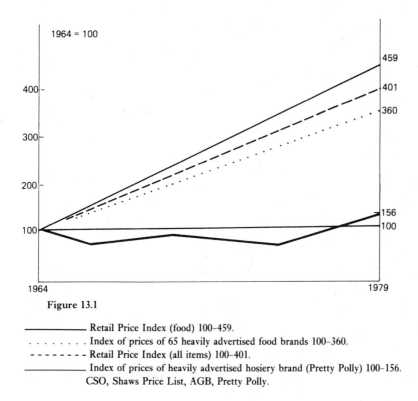

Figure 13.1

———————— Retail Price Index (food) 100–459.
. . . . Index of prices of 65 heavily advertised food brands 100–360.
- - - - - - - Retail Price Index (all items) 100–401.
———————— Index of prices of heavily advertised hosiery brand (Pretty Polly) 100–156.
CSO, Shaws Price List, AGB, Pretty Polly.

APPENDIX: CORPORATE CAMPAIGN IN THE REPUBLIC OF IRELAND

Pretty Polly has sold modest quantities of hosiery in the Republic of Ireland for over 30 years. Virtually no specific advertising in support of the brand had even been made, the company relying upon a degree of 'fall-out' from UK publications and advertising to give some awareness of Pretty Polly.

Sales in the prestige branded sector of the Irish market were approximately 9000 dozen per week, of which Pretty Polly accounted for 1200 dozen per week (or 13 per cent) in 1979.

In the Autumn of 1979 it was decided the Irish market was capable of significant penetration if a real effort were made to cover the country with an expanded sales effort by our distributor, backed by a national advertising campaign.

Starting at the end of January 1980 with some 80 major outdoor poster sites, booked for one year, colour pages in four women's magazines and a 30-second radio spot campaign, the effect was dramatic. Sales in Quarter

1 are up by 83 per cent and currently are over 100 per cent up in April, at a sales rate of 3000 dozen per week. New accounts opened have exceeded 250, increasing the existing 500 accounts prior to the advertising campaign by 50 per cent.

The total cost of the campaign is estimated to be £130 000 for the whole year. It is conservatively estimated that our year-end sales will have produced over £200 000 extra profit, which will pay for the entire advertising campaign and leave £70 000 as net gain. Our long-term position is immensely strengthened with Pretty Polly attaining 30 per cent of the prestige market and poised for another leap forward in 1981, when a similar, but larger, campaign is scheduled to consolidate our position of leadership.

Section Three

Direct Response,
Consumer Goods and Services

14

The Launch of Tjaereborg Rejser

BACKGROUND

Tjaereborg Rejser were founded in 1950 by a Danish pastor! They are now the third largest package holiday tour operator in Europe.

Their growth is based on the simple proposition of selling high quality holidays at prices significantly below other tour operators. The cost saving is achieved primarily by selling direct to the consumer, saving ten to fifteen per cent in travel agent's commission.

The UK was a logical place for Tjaereborg to launch as it is the largest source of package holiday takers in Europe, and a market in which direct sell was embryonic. BMP were appointed in June 1977, and the company officially opened for business on 1st January 1978.

THE BRITISH HOLIDAY MARKET

The package holiday market is a volatile and highly fragmented one. 1972 and 1973 were peak years for the industry with over four and a half million holidays sold each year, but economic recession, the loss of confidence in tour operators following the collapse of Courtline, and the hot summers of 1974 and 1976 had led to a gradual decline in the market.

There were already over a hundred tour operators fighting for a share of this shrinking market, from the giant mainstream companies like Thompsons and Cosmos, to the small specialist outfits like Kuoni and Inghams.

In their first season Tjaereborg aimed to sell 25 000 holidays to consumers in the South East. In 1977 there were 1.3 million package holiday takers from this part of the country, so Tjaereborg were targeting for a modest 2 per cent share. However, as their programme concentrated on popular destinations such as Spain and Majorca, a sector in which there was severe overcapacity and fierce competition, it was evident that without their strong proposition they would have been foolish to enter the market at all.

THE ROLE OF ADVERTISING

Figures 14.1 and 14.2 illustrate the differences in method of operation between a conventional tour operator and a direct-sell tour operator.

Conventional tour operators use travel agents to distribute their brochures, and rely on

155

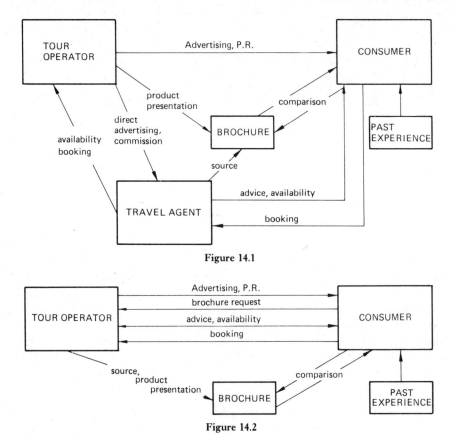

Figure 14.1

Figure 14.2

them to recommend their holidays to consumers when asked for advice. Travel agents also take bookings and collect money for conventional tour operators. The role of advertising is simply to persuade the consumer to consider that operator when choosing a holiday. It is not necessary for the advertising to inform consumers how to go about booking their holiday.

To purchase a holiday from a direct-sell tour operator, the consumer must contact the tour operator to get a brochure, and again to ask for advice or information, and again to make the booking. This is obviously more complex than dropping in on a local travel agent. The advertising thus has the dual role of creating demand and also telling the consumer how to satisfy that demand.

Figure 14.3 illustrates the important stages in the direct-sell booking claim and the role of advertising in each stage.

  (i)   The advertising must motivate consumers to request a brochure and inform them
        how to do so.
 (ii)   The consumer will compare the brochure with competitors' brochures, so it must be
        consistent with the advertising claims.
(iii)   Holidays are a very expensive purchase and consumers are very suspicious of tour
        operators following the collapse of several notable tour operators in the mid-seventies.
        At the stage when consumers are actually committing themselves, the advertising has

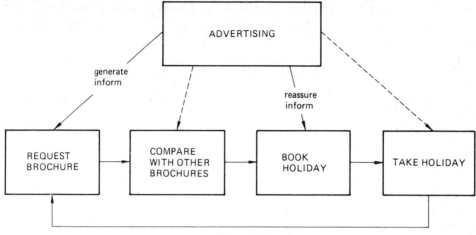

Figure 14.3

a vital role in providing reassurance about the experience and reliability of this new company.

This 'schema' provides the structure for the evaluation of the Tjaereborg launch advertising.

ADVERTISING DEVELOPMENT

Qualitative research was carried out to discover the important factors in planning and booking a holiday and consumers' reactions to the Tjaereborg proposition.

Respondents varied markedly in the thoroughness and degree of premeditation involved in planning and booking their holiday. However, it was evident that, having decided where to go and the standard of facilities required, price was the key factor in deciding which tour operator to travel with.

Not surprisingly, therefore, low price was the primary attraction of the Tjaereborg proposition. Pretesting of the initial executions, however, showed that low price alone tended to imply poor quality, a reaction heightened by the general distrust of tour operators. The best way of reassuring consumers about the quality of the holiday was by a factual explanation of how the low price is achieved. In other words, to say that by cutting out the travel agent, and thus his commission, it was possible to offer holidays of comparable quality to other tour operators, but at prices at least ten per cent cheaper.

No demographic groups stood out as particularly likely to book a Tjaereborg holiday. Inexperienced holiday takers were loath to pioneer an unknown company with a novel booking method, and thus it seemed that the discriminators of potential Tjaereborg bookers would be attitudinal rather than demographic. The target market was therefore defined as all package holiday takers, a group which is biased towards ABC1s and 16 to 44 year olds.

A mixed media schedule was used. Television was included for impact and because of the prestige attached to advertisers in that medium. The primary role of press was brochure generation, and publications with a good history of direct response were chosen for the schedule. In addition the press advertisements provided increased coverage of the primary target group, more information about Tjaereborg and a detailed explanation of the booking method. The total media budget was £83 000. The television advertising was on London and Southern during January 1978; the press insertions carried on until the end of February.

EVALUATING THE ADVERTISING

As mentioned above, the section on advertising evaluation will follow the structure outlined in Figure 14.3.

Generating Brochure Requests

AWARENESS OF TJAEREBORG

A necessary precursor to entering the booking chain is to be aware of its existence. Table 14.1 shows the results of a post-advertising awareness check of 1100 adults.

TABLE 14.1: POST-ADVERTISING AWARENESS OF TJAEREBORG

	Expenditure[3] (£)	Share of voice[4] %	Prompted awareness %
Tjaereborg (1978)	115 200	8.1	32[1]
Vingressor (1979)	196 600	8.3	17[2]

[1] Respondents intending to holiday in 1978.
[2] Respondents who have taken a foreign holiday in the last five years.
[3] MEAL.
[4] Share of 'foreign tours and holidays'.

By March 1978 32 per cent of the holiday-taking public in the South East were aware of Tjaereborg. In the same survey Thomsons, Cosmos and Cooks achieved scores of ninety plus, which is to be expected given their brand share and length of time in the market. A better comparison is with the prompted awareness achieved by Vingressor, a Swedish direct-sell company, after their UK launch in 1979.

A post-awareness check carried out in March 1979 showed that Vingressor had only 17 per cent prompted awareness, slightly over half that of Tjaereborg, despite a similar share of voice (MEAL has been used for expenditure and share of voice because of the importance of press in both launches; Tjaereborg's press/TV expenditure was split 50:50, Vingressor's 57:43) and, allowing for inflation, a 40 per cent increase in media spend.

Vingressor had the disadvantage of being second into the market. Tjaereborg's novelty, not to say notoriety, within the travel trade meant that they received considerable coverage in industry publications, consumer press and holiday programmes. This would undoubtedly have boosted awareness of Tjaereborg considerably, but, as Table 14.2 shows, advertising was still the primary awareness generator for Tjaereborg.

The post-advertising awareness check also showed that awareness of Tjaereborg was higher amongst the main target group, and moreover that ABC1s were much more likely than C2DEs to have heard of Tjaereborg first through a press advertisement, one of the intentions of the mixed media schedule.

TABLE 14.2: HOW WAS TJAEREBORG FIRST
HEARD OF? BASE: ALL AWARE OF TJAEREBORG

TV advertisement	66%
Press advertisement	11%
TV programme	10%
Newspaper article	3%
Friends/relatives	4%
On the radio	3%
Others	8%

Fieldwork International Awareness check, March
1978.

BROCHURE GENERATION

Table 14.3 shows the number of brochure requests generated by each medium.

Television is apparently more efficient than the press at generating brochures. This is undoubtedly exaggerated as the Ansaphone number was printed on the press advertisements and thus some Ansaphone responses would actually have been generated by the press.

TABLE 14.3: BROCHURE REQUESTS BY MEDIA, JANUARY/FEBRUARY 1978

Media	Expenditure (£) (actual)	Number of responses	Cost per response (pence)
London	31 637	57 053	55
Southern	10 154	9 898	103
Total TV (Ansaphone)	41 791	66 651	62
Press (coupon)	41 177	57 290	72
Total	82 968	124 241	67

More surprising is the difference in efficiency between London and Southern, with Southern roughly twice as expensive per brochure generated as London. The reasons for this are not fully understood. Although London received 70 more adult TVRs than Southern (398 against 328), the cost per thousand was identical. A partial explanation is probably that the incidence of package holiday taking is 50 per cent higher amongst Londoners than Southerners (BNTS).

There are no directly comparable response data available on either press or TV as there were no comparable advertisers. However, Thames TV have provided anonymous data about their five most successful holiday advertisers to give a yardstick against which to measure Tjaereborg's success. Table 14.4 compares these responses with the weight of the exposure of the five heaviest advertisers (there were only six major advertisers on Thames in 1978 excluding Tjaereborg). While Tjaereborg account for 8 per cent of these advertisers' total adult TVRs, they account for 48 per cent of their total brochure requests. On average the other advertisers generated 13 brochure requests per TVR; the Tjaereborg advertisement generated 143 requests per TVR.

It has been emphasized that these comparisons are quite crude because a mainstream holiday advertiser does not *need* to generate direct brochure requests through its advertising. However, when consumers do ring up to request a brochure they are told that they

TABLE 14.4: WEIGHT OF EXPOSURE AND NUMBER OF BROCHURE REQUESTS OF FIVE ANONYMOUS
HOLIDAY ADVERTISERS, LONDON, JANUARY/FEBRUARY 1978

	Weight of exposure (adult TVRs)	Number of brochure requests
A	1 610	20 765
B	1 093	17 974
C	949	11 534
D	617	8 928
E	494	2 273
Tjaereborg	398	57 053

Note: Except in the case of Tjaereborg, the numbers in the two columns are not necessarily related to their opposite numbers.

are allowed to ask for up to six brochures. It is significant that, when in a position to obtain a brochure by simply uttering a name, rather than walking down to a travel agent, 70 per cent of consumers who rang up for a Tjaereborg brochure asked *only* for that brochure. That this is the case, when choice is so facile, is an interesting demonstration of the power of Tjaereborg's commercial, and of Tjaereborg's proposition.

Low price was identified as the key element in the advertising strategy, and in fact a postal survey of 1000 brochure requestors, 416 of whom replied (Table 14.5), showed that low price was the most memorable communication of the commercial and the key reason for requesting a brochure.

TABLE 14.5: POSTAL SURVEY OF 1000 BROCHURE REQUESTORS

	State anything you can remember about the advertisements you saw for Tjaereborg (%)	
	TV	Press
Lower price/cheaper than other companies	45	32
Book direct/no travel agent's fee	37	26
Phone number	10	7
Just the name	2	10

	State the main reason you sent off for a Tjaereborg brochure (%)
Inexpensive/cheaper holidays/lower prices	39
Wanted to compare prices/services	23
No travel agents/direct selling	13
Wanted to see what holidays were offered	10

Fieldwork International 1978 Postal Survey.

Brochure Comparisons

The brochure is a very important, in some ways the most important, part of the overall communication from Tjaereborg to the consumer. Obviously the advertising can have no direct effect on consumers when they are comparing the brochures of different companies. However, the brochure must be consistent, in image and tone of voice, with the advertising.

To cut the cost of your holiday, cut out the travel agent.

Would you like to save 10% on the cost of your holiday?

Like £35 on a fortnight's holiday for two in Majorca?

Or £60 on a holiday in Greece?

These are the sort of savings you can make by cutting out the travel agent and booking your holiday direct with Tjaereborg.

Tjaereborg are one of Europe's biggest holiday companies, and starting this summer, they'll be taking British holidaymakers to Europe's most popular resorts.

Although Tjaereborg save you money, you won't have to give up any quality.

In fact, Tjaereborg share many of their hotels with companies that charge considerably more for the same holiday.

And all Tjaereborg's prices are guaranteed, there are no hidden charges, and there won't be any surcharges.

If you'd like to save money on your holiday, all you have to do is pick one from the Tjaereborg brochure, and book it direct, either by phoning or calling in at the Tjaereborg office.

To get your free Tjaereborg brochure, send off the coupon or phone 01-493 7232.

To cut out the travel agent, cut out the coupon.

NAME_____

_____ (BLOCK CAPITALS)

ADDRESS_____

◆ TJAEREBORG
7–8 Conduit Street, London, W.I.

Tjaereborg press advertisement.

To ensure that this was the case the brochure was researched at the same time as the advertising; consequently it has some unusual features. The shape is landscape rather than portrait, which helps emphasize the uniqueness of Tjaereborg. The copy about hotels and resorts points out problems and faults as well as advantages, thus making Tjaereborg stand out as particularly trustworthy and honest. Finally the prices are clearly marked and 'no surcharges' is guaranteed, thus reinforcing the price claims made in the advertising.

The returns from the postal survey showed that in fact 90 per cent of brochure requestors thought that the Tjaereborg brochure was as good as or better than its competitors.

Conversion to Bookers

The final stage in the booking chain is for the consumer to ring up Tjaereborg and actually book the holiday. As the consumer is at this point committing himself to large sums of money he/she must be fairly sure that Tjaereborg are reliable and trustworthy. If in fact the advertising is effective in reassuring consumers it should be possible to demonstrate that brochure requestors exposed to the advertising are more likely to convert to bookers than requestors not exposed to it.

There were a significant number of brochure requests from outside mainstream TV-advertised areas, due in part to those press insertions which were national or semi-national, but otherwise due, presumably, to national PR exposure.

Table 14.6 shows the conversion to booking ratio in TV-advertised and non-TV-advertised areas. The ratio of brochure requestors to bookers was ten to one in the former and

TABLE 14.6: CONVERSION OF BROCHURE REQUESTORS TO BOOKERS

	Number of brochure requests	Number of bookers[1]	Conversion ratio
Main advertised areas (London and South East)	94 012	9 573	9.8:1
Rest of England	27 319	1 202	22.7:1
Other areas (Scotland, Wales and overseas)	1 026	225	4.6:1
Total non-advertised areas	28 345	1 427	19.9:1

[1] 2.6 holidays per booker
2 to 3 per cent of data lost due to misaddressing.

twenty to one in the latter. Thus consumers with Tjaereborg brochures exposed to a reasonably heavy weight of advertising were apparently twice as likely to book a holiday with Tjaereborg than those who had not.

However, there is another possible explanation for these findings. In 1978 all Tjaereborg holidays departed from Gatwick airport. By and large the advertised areas are nearer to Gatwick than the non-advertised areas. In other words it could be that the product was inhibiting brochure requestors from outside the TV-advertised areas from booking, rather than the advertising encouraging bookings within the advertised areas.

To control out the product variable, the conversion ratios in six counties which are roughly equidistant from Gatwick and which all have London between them and Gatwick have been compared. Of the six counties – which are Hertfordshire, Essex, Buckingham-shire, Berkshire, Oxfordshire and Bedfordshire – two, namely Oxfordshire and Bedford-shire, fall substantially outside the London and Southern ITV areas.

As Table 14.7 shows, the conversion ratios in the advertised areas is 13 to one, whereas in the non-advertised areas it is 22 to one. This is substantial evidence that the advertising is having an influence on the final stage of the booking claim.

TABLE 14.7: CONVERSION OF BROCHURE REQUESTORS TO BOOKERS BY COUNTY

County	Number of brochure requests	Number of bookers	Conversion ratio
Hertfordshire	7 695	574	13.4:1
Essex	18 212	1 265	14.4:1
Buckinghamshire	2 180	206	10.6:1
Berkshire	2 822	328	8.6:1
Total advertised	30 910	2 373	13.0:1
Oxfordshire	2 052	69	29.7:1
Bedfordshire	1 796	106	16.9:1
Total non-advertised	3 848	175	22.0:1

WAS THE ADVERTISING EFFECTIVE?

In answer to this question, so far this chapter has looked at the mechanism of the advertising and evaluated it against such criteria as are available and seem sensible.

One fact not yet mentioned is that, although Tjaereborg targeted to sell 25 000 holidays, they actually sold 29 000, thus going 16 per cent over budget. It could be argued that this is, per se, a demonstration of advertising effectiveness. However, it also could be argued that the direct-sell operation, and the advertising which is so integral to it, was not the most cost-effective way of marketing Tjaereborg's holidays, and that a conventional operation could have been equally successful and more cost-effective.

Direct Sell

Table 14.8 lists all the marketing costs which Tjaereborg had during their first season in the UK. Apart from the cost of advertising (media and production) most of the costs relate to the printing and distribution of brochures.

The net sales value (NSV) of the 29 000 holidays which Tjaereborg sold in 1978 was £3 500 000. At £251 000 the advertising and distribution costs were 7.2 per cent of NSV.

TABLE 14.8: DIRECT SELL COSTS (£)

Advertising	83 000
Production	68 000
200 000 brochures	57 000
Postage and packaging	32 000
Handling house	4 000
Ansaphone costs	7 000
Total	251 000

BMP Estimates.

Conventional

Table 14.9 estimates the costs of marketing these same 29 000 holidays using the conventional brochures distribution mechanism through travel agents.

No advertising other than trade press is costed in, although it could be argued that a moderate amount of advertising would be advisable. However, as Tjaereborg's holidays would be such good value for money they could probably rely on consumers finding them

TABLE 14.9: CONVENTIONAL COSTS (£)

Advertising	5 000	(trade press)
Production	2 000	(trade press)
300 000 brochures	78 000	
Sales force (8)	35 000	
Launch	10 000	
Travel agents' com.	350 000	
Total	480 000	

BMP Estimates.

out for themselves and hope that travel agents would reassure consumers about their quality. A vigorous trade press campaign and a prestigious trade launch would be necessary!

There are approximately 1700 travel agents in the South East; however it would not be necessary to service them all, probably the 500 largest would suffice. A well known tour operator employs a sales force of eight and prints 300 000 brochures to cover just such a number of travel agents and the costs for Tjaereborg are based on this.

The largest new cost would be travel agents' commission, which would represent at least ten per cent of the net sales value of the holidays. The total cost of this option is therefore £480 000, which is 13.7 per cent of NSV.

The conventional operation is almost twice as expensive as selling direct, which means that Tjaereborg would have had to sell a considerably higher volume of holidays through travel agents than the 29 000 they sold direct to the consumer to make as much money.

Tjaereborg could pass on the cost of the travel agent to the consumer as do all other tour operators. It appears that if they sold 29 000 holidays this way, they would make more money as there would be no expensive media costs to bear. However, this line of reasoning is invalid as to raise the price of Tjaereborg's holidays would destroy their proposition. To sell their holidays in this situation Tjaereborg would have to segment the market on a different basis than price. For example, they could offer unusual destinations or specialize in certain destinations, though given the mainstream nature of their programme this is not really feasible. Alternatively they could build a proposition around high quality; however, for a new company this in itself would require substantial advertising support, which would be competing head on with the big tour operators without the benefits of their long established and reliable brand names.

As discussed in the introduction it is apparent that if Tjaereborg had not had a distinctive proposition, i.e. low price, they would have been foolhardy to enter the UK holiday market at all. Now it has been demonstrated that direct sell, and the advertising which is such a vital ingredient in direct sell, was by far the most cost-effective way for Tjaereborg to sell their holidays.

SUMMARY OF THE ARGUMENT

Tjaereborg had a requirement to sell 25 000 holidays; they had a mainstream programme of resorts but a distinctive proposition, namely, lower prices achieved by their means of operation – selling direct to the consumer.

Price was the key element in the advertisements which were developed for Tjaereborg. The television commercial used the distinctive 'How much?' device, while the press concentrated on giving consumers information about the quality of the holidays and the size and experience of the company.

There are three stages in the holiday booking chain: (i) brochure requesting, (ii) brochure comparison, (iii) booking the holiday. It has been argued that advertising has a major influence on (i) and (iii).

The scale of the number of requests generated by the television advertising has been demonstrated by comparison with other holiday advertisers; it was, simply, unprecedented. Moreover the percentage of solus requests has been used as evidence of the degree of interest aroused by the advertising.

The importance of the advertising in reassuring consumers that Tjaereborg are a trust-worthy company at the stage at which they are booking a holiday has been demonstrated by comparing the conversion ratios of advertised and non-advertised counties which are equidistant from Gatwick.

Finally, the cost-effectiveness of the advertising has been demonstrated by contrasting the costs and profits of the direct-sell method with the conventional operating system. It is clear that Tjaereborg would have had to sell a considerably higher volume of holidays to achieve the same return if the latter system had been used. In fact, as it was, they sold 16 per cent more holidays than they had originally budgeted to do.

DISCUSSION AND CONCLUSIONS

This case history is direct response because advertising is the means of the advertiser carrying out his business as well as the tool used for creating demand for his products. It differs from most direct-response advertisers in that with Tjaereborg a brand is being created.

The launch of Tjaereborg was the launch of a new sector of the travel industry, and it is important to establish Tjaereborg as number one in that category. The benefit of this is that with repeat bookings and increased personal recommendation from satisfied customers the need for advertising decreases over the years, making the whole operation even more profitable. This contrasts with the lot of the conventional tour operators, where the travel agents' commission is omnipresent.

When seeking to demonstrate the effectiveness of Tjaereborg's advertising it could be argued that the advertising should have generated even more brochure requests or achieved an even lower conversion ratio. However, given the finite number of holidays to sell, and even here Tjaereborg over-achieved, this argument is impossible to validate.

The difficulties of demonstrating anything at all in the real world are immense. Without areas controlled for such variables as PR, distance from Gatwick, media weight, propensity to take package holidays and so on, it is difficult to take these factors into account and impossible validly to assign causes to effects. However, the criteria of the business man are not the same as those of the empirical scientist. The fact that Tjaereborg were successful, and continue to be so, despite the opposition of the travel industry and their dire predictions of doom for Tjaereborg, setting up in such difficult times, is perhaps the best demonstration of advertising effectiveness which could be offered.

15

The British Film Institute and Advertising Effectiveness

MARKET BACKGROUND

The British Film Institute was founded in 1933 and is funded by the Department of Education and Science. Its purpose is 'to encourage the development of the art of the film, to promote its use as a record of contemporary life and manners and to foster public appreciation of it from these points of view' (BFI Charter). In this connection, the BFI opened the National Film Theatre in 1952, and expanded to two cinemas on the South bank of the Thames in the late 1960s.

In addition to the NFT, the BFI undertakes the operation of the following activities:

1. Educational Advisory Services
2. Film Production Board
3. Television Archive
4. National Film Archive
5. Information and Documentation
6. Regional Department
7. Film Availability Service
8. Editorial Department

The British Film Institute is thus a *unique* organization in the world of cinema and television.

People can become associated with the BFI in a number of different ways: (a) as student members, (b) as associate members, (c) as full members, and (d) as corporate members.

The memberships differ in cost and administrative rights. All forms of membership entitle one to purchase tickets at the NFT, have access to the full range of BFI services including the NFT's bars, restaurant and bookshop, receive a copy of the monthly bulletin and purchase tickets for the London Film Festival. The full membership also entitles one to receive *Sight and Sound*, the BFI's magazine published quarterly. Above all, membership entitles one to see as many of the 20 000 + films shown at the NFT every year as possible – the greatest number at any cinema complex.

In 1979, the British Film Institute had 33 433 members in all. The proportion of membership was 12 758 full (38 per cent) and 20 675 associate (62 per cent) (including students, who are 16 per cent of all members). However, the number of new members joining the BFI had stagnated over the last few years. BFI membership figures indicated the growth in new members was not keeping the NFT theatres filled and that *something* had to be accomplished to recruit new members.

OBJECTIVES OF THE CAMPAIGN

In March 1979 the British Film Institute retained Ogilvy and Mather Ltd as its advertising agency. The role of the agency was to aid in developing current members and in attracting new members. To accomplish these objectives, OBM proposed a press advertising campaign aimed at recruiting associate members (the cost of this being about half that of full membership). Early in these discussions, it was decided to use the NFT as the 'flagship' of the BFI's membership drive.

It was written into the campaign's objectives that at least 80 per cent of the BFI's advertising expenditure should be recovered by the incoming revenue directly attributable to the advertising. All executions carried a coupon and were scrupulously monitored by OBM and the BFI. Response per advertisement, and per medium, were compared in the classical manner for evaluating the press direct response advertising.

Apart from the occasional 'ad hoc' advertisement, this was the first recruiting campaign the BFI had ever done. The agency started with assumptions and hypothesis developed in conjunction with the BFI, and gradually, as knowledge of the advertising tasks became more tangible, the campaign successfully evolved.

THE BFI AND THE COMPETITION

In the broadest sense, the BFI's competition comes from all leisure activities in London which also attract frequent film goers – such as reading, listening to music, going to the theatre, concerts, opera, restaurants, pubs, museums, etc., and, more specifically, other cinemas. With the exception of the London Film Festival, the NFT does not show first-run films, so it is not a *direct* competitor of the West End or local cinemas but is a direct competitor with 'art' or independent cinemas: the NFT shows thousands of films from all countries, from all areas of cinema.

A quantitative research project by OBM showed that BFI members claim to attend the cinema very frequently. In fact, the frequency of *claimed* visits to the cinema exceeds one every two weeks on average.

The study also made it clear that the competitive leisure pursuits of the type of person attracted to the BFI were extensive but were primarily *interior* ones which involved the senses of sight and sound, such as reading, listening to music and going to the theatre.

CAMPAIGN DEVELOPMENT

The First Stage of the Campaign

The first execution was developed solely from the BFI's brief to the agency. This included reference to the location of the NFT (a map), a discussion of the rights of members to use

BFI facilities, pictures of the clubroom and restaurant, a discussion of famous people who had given lectures at the NFT, and a picture of *Sight and Sound* and the NFT monthly programme. The primary message was that one should join the NFT, for it is 'One of the biggest and best cinema clubs in the world'.

The first campaign was also speculative from the media point of view. Educated guesses about the membership produced a wide range of media choices, some of which proved cost effective and others not (Table 15.2)*

TABLE 15.2: MEDIA CHOICES OF FIRST CAMPAIGN

Publication	Space cost £	No. of cheques	£	No. of details requested	£s from requests
Guardian	1402	122	586	187	
LAM	162	5	24	11	
Time Out	351	54	259	48	
Evening Standard	2720	132	634	123	
New Statesman	344	15	12	20	
The Observer	1020	294	1411	292	
Private Eye	637	59	283	37	
Totals	6637	680	3264	718	354

The results of the first stage of the campaign (Table 15.1), completed in the absence of objective data, were regarded as quite encouraging to the BFI and OBM, particularly if one discounts the test media which were ineffective and one assumes that the income gained from a newly recruited member *exceeds* that of an initial subscription (for new members will attend the NFT several times in a year and are quite likely to renew subscriptions next year). Also, this figure reflects *only* those responding directly to the coupon. The additional indirect response must have been substantial, but this was not measured.

TABLE 15.1: FIRST CAMPAIGN (SPRING 1979)

No. recruited	Advertising costs £	Direct revenue £	+ or − £
776[a]	5666	3725	− 1941

[a] These figures include a number of students recruited by student publications not included in the media effectiveness table.

With a further 72 members converting from 718 requests for information (10 per cent rate) another £354 was generated, bringing the total revenue generated to £3618. The most cost-effective media were the *Observer*, the *Guardian* and *Time Out*.

So while the first campaign did not pay for itself solely by the income it created, great

* At this very early stage, it was agreed that a large scale survey should be conducted of members of the BFI to help answer questions on current members' behaviour and attitudes for the purpose of developing future advertising.

'Last year a small select audience saw 2,000 films here.'

‹ Because I'm often working on location, I miss a lot of good films when they do the circuit.

Lots of busy people have the same problem. That's one reason why it makes sense to belong to the British Film Institute.

You get another chance to see the best examples of the popular cinema when they're included in an NFT season. You also get to see the sort of films that just aren't shown anywhere else.

The choice is amazing, nearly forty films every week. And you get a monthly programme in advance so you can plan what you want to see, and when.

It's the most civilised way to watch movies – you can get a drink or have something to eat all under the same roof.

If you take cinema seriously, you should join the British Film Institute. And stop missing out on good films. ›

John Hurt

Take advantage of our immediate membership scheme today!

Post to: Membership Dept. GD3, British Film Institute,
    81 Dean Street, London W1.

I ENCLOSE £4.80. Please make me an associate member of the British Film Institute, entitling me to purchase tickets for the NFT, with up to three guests, use of licensed bar, clubroom and restaurant, illustrated NFT programme brochure, BFI News sheet and advanced booking for the London Film Festival.

Name _____

Address _____

FREE copy of Sight and Sound when you use this coupon to join the British Film Institute.

bfi The National Film Theatre
     The British Film Institute

British Film Institute press advertisement.

hopes were held for the next campaign which would be guided by a membership survey proposed by OBM to define the target market and its needs.

The Second Stage of the Campaign

In order to create the most effective advertising, OBM commissioned a quantitative postal market research project among BFI members to determine the characteristics of the target audience: demographic data, usership data, media data and some attitudinal data were collected.

The results of this research revealed a clear picture of current members. OBM believed that high potential members should share many of the characteristics of current members and therefore assumed the data collected about current members could be used in constructing messages to high potential members. An advertising plan was then drafted to aid in creative development by employing these data.

Members are, in the main, men living in London, of an average of 35 years old, from the upper socio-economic grades, with a high level of educational achievement, single, and living with friends, relatives or alone. They are also readers of the *Observer*, the *Guardian* and *Time Out*. Differences between the three basic types of member were notable, and these differences were taken into account when forming the creative strategy.

Although there may have been some overclaiming by respondents in the frequency of cinema visits, the cinema plays an integral role in the lives of current members and would play such a role with potential members. Research suggests that potential members know about the BFI and will have visited the NFT (many current members made their first visit to NFT as a guest of a member).

Attracted by both the *social* aspect of film viewing (the experience of going with friends for a date to the cinema and enjoying the bar and restaurant) and the *private* enjoyment of film viewing, it was thought that potential members would be stimulated by emphasis on both these aspects. BFI members enjoyed other activities which combined the *social* and *private*, *sight* and/or *sound*, in indoor activity such as concerts, visits to museums, etc.

Because of their educational and socio-economic background and activities, potential members are part of an 'elite', though some may not recognize they are or even reject the suggestion. However, *selectivity* in film was thought to be an acceptable form of elitism with members and potential members.

Much that was learned from this survey made the second campaign more single minded than the first, and consequently more successful. Firstly, most potential members (like current members) know where the NFT is before they join. Secondly, they are attracted primarily to using the NFT and are not necessarily attracted to or aware of the other services of the BFI. Thirdly, stress on knowledge of a combination of popular and somewhat esoteric films is more relevant to our target audience than a stress on popular films alone.

From the research, the agency concluded that a potential member would be attracted to a message from a person involved in the film industry exhorting them to join the select company of BFI members. John Hurt was thought to be an appropriate choice, with the right appeal to young, intelligent film goers, due to his participation in both very popular films (*Alien*) and somewhat more esoteric films and television plays (*Midnight Express*, *Quentin Crisp*). The fact that he is British and a BFI member was also important for the credibility of his testimony.

The research also suggested strongly to the agency that high potential members know about the BFI, have probably been to the NFT, and are even likely to have friends or relatives who are members. It was hypothesized that a strong *reminder* of the NFT and an inducement to join could reach these high potential members. Therefore, a Large Coupon advertisement was developed to reach these individuals, as an alternative to the 'testimonial' advertisement.

The two advertisements derived from these strategies were placed in the media that had proved most effective previously.

From the advertising test, it was apparent that the Large Coupon advertisement was *not* drawing as well as the John Hurt testimonial (Table 15.3).

TABLE 15.3: COMPARATIVE RESULTS OF THE DIFFERENT COPY USED

	Members recruited	Cost £	Revenue £	Cost/recruit £
Black Lagoon	811	6750	3862	8.32
Large Coupon	440	3074	2122	6.98
John Hurt	511	2210	2452	4.32
Total	1762	11 934	8436	

The John Hurt testimonial paid for itself, and Autumn 1979 produced a surplus of £242 (11 per cent over total cost); it cost £4.32 to recruit a member. In contrast, Black Lagoon 'lost' £2888 (if one examines only direct cost) and it cost £8.32 to recruit a member. The Large Coupon 'lost' £952 (if one examines only the direct cost) and it cost £6.98 to recruit a member.

THE JOHN HURT TESTIMONIAL

The John Hurt testimonial was therefore chosen to run in February 1980.

In this test, the John Hurt advertisement proved a stunning success. It produced £6059 in direct recruitment profit and the cost per member recruited was £1.97 (Table 15.4).

Thus, by employing a proper planning procedure, a discriminating media selection and a relevant creative approach, the campaign succeeded.

TABLE 15.4: JOHN HURT TESTIMONIAL

No. recruited	Advertisement costs £	Revenue £	+ or − £
2151	4256	10 315	+ 6059

HOW SUCCESSFUL THE CAMPAIGN ACTUALLY IS

It must be emphasized that the *direct response* (which has been measured) is not the only response upon which the success of this campaign should be assessed. Other factors must be taken into account.

1. If the newly recruited members behave as existing members themselves claim, they will each visit the NFT 10 times a year, which will generate £24 extra income. They will also buy drinks at the bar, eat at the restaurant, etc.
2. The new members are more than likely to renew their membership for at least one more year.
3. While there is no way of measuring the number of people who joined BFI as an indirect result of seeing this advertisement, undoubtedly a number of new members joined in this way.
4. There is no way of determining how a new member's relationship with the BFI will develop or the positive effect the advertisement had on limiting the rate of BFI member attrition.
5. New members contribute to the recruiting of other new members by word of mouth and 'member get member' programmes. So the recruiting of one new member can bring in another, free of charge.

If one takes only the first two points and makes conservative assumptions derived from the research mentioned previously, the following picture is revealed in Table 15.5.

TABLE 15.5: SUCCESS OF THE TESTIMONIAL

New members	2151
5 NFT visits/year at £1.20[a] for two years on their own	£12
Direct income	£24 012
Cost of associate membership	£4.80
Average length of membership	1.5 more years[b]
Indirect income	£15 487

[a] Half the number of times current members claim.
[b] Half the length of time current associate members in the membership survey claim to stay members.

Taking into account direct income and the first two aspects of indirect income generation, the John Hurt campaign can be expected to produce the revenue shown in Table 15.6.

TABLE 15.6: EXPECTED REVENUE FROM CAMPAIGN

	Revenue £
Direct from coupon	6 059
5 visits yearly × 2 years	24 012
1.5 years additional membership	15 487
Total	45 558

CONCLUSION

The campaign entry – the John Hurt testimonial – produced a direct recruitment profit of £6059 (excluding agency preparation and production charges) and an indirect profit of many thousands more, if one takes into account the fact that BFI membership involves a great deal of related revenue generation.

The 1979–80 campaign succeeded in increasing the number of associate BFI members by 3913 directly attributable to the advertising (coupon replies), at a direct profit of £2791 and an indirect one of many thousands more (Table 15.7).

TABLE 15.7: GRAND TOTAL

No. recruited	Advertising space costs £	Revenue £	+ or − £
3913	15 950	18 741	+ 2791

16

Royal Air Force Officer Recruitment

BACKGROUND

It is of primary importance to the defence of our country against potential aggressors that our Armed Forces are kept at full strength. Thus there is a continual need to recruit men and women for commissioned service in the Royal Air Force.

The RAF is not a career which comes immediately to mind for most young people thinking about a job. It is a discrete world, with relatively remote airbases and security restrictions which inhibit public contact. Thus few young people have ever met an RAF Officer.

There will always be some young people, many with Service backgrounds, whose lifelong ambition is to become a pilot with the RAF. But this source of supply goes only a very small way to maintain the steady flow of high quality recruits needed to keep establishments up to strength.

A variety of background factors affect recruitment to any walk of life, and the RAF is no exception. The employer has control over some, but not over others. The latter category includes the overall supply pool; what competitors are offering; and negative publicity about the job in question. The main controllable factors are the terms and conditions of service offered; the qualities and qualifications required of candidates; the nature of the jobs available; and the volume and nature of the information published about them.

Advertising is the main vehicle for this last category, supplemented by a network of Careers Information Offices throughout the country, by a limited number of service liaison officers at schools and universities (whose own careers advisers are a strong and not necessarily beneficial influence) and by other points of public contact such as air shows and RAF open days (which mainly reach those who are already converted).

But it is RAF advertising that reaches more young people more efficiently and more quickly than any other recruiting aid.

The positive and negative effects on recruitment of the factors mentioned are almost impossible to disentangle and measure, but we submit that the variable of the advertising input can be demonstrated to bear a direct relationship with recruitment achievement, in terms of both quantity and quality.

ADVERTISING OBJECTIVES

The role of advertising is to produce, as economically as possible, high quality candidates for commissioned service in the Royal Air Force in sufficient quantity to fill given numbers of vacancies.

The total requirement embraces both aircrew and ground branches, involving a wide variety of specialists. For the purpose of this submission we are focusing on the officer aircrew recruitment task, which has the highest priority, is relatively straightforward and exemplifies the total task.

The primary target group for aircrew is young men, 17 to 25 years old, at point of job choice, with at least 5 'O' levels at Grade C or above. In addition aircrew candidates must have flying aptitudes – an inherent quality possessed by an individual that can be identified only by special tests.

The strategy for aircrew advertising is to highlight flying and aircraft, which we know from research to be the main appeal of the RAF to our target group, and to reassure them about their ability to cope, after training, with the demanding nature of the job.

Most of them need this reassurance, and doubt their own ability to match up to the exacting demands of the job, and to fit into the unknown elitist society which an RAF Officers' Mess represents to them.

DESCRIPTION OF THE CAMPAIGN

The officer aircrew campaign aims to present an irresistible picture of flying with the Royal Air Force using dramatic photography of modern military aircraft in flight. It aims to make the dream achievable and not alien by making them feel that existing pilots are human and were just like them initially; the copy emphasizes that you never know if you can do it until you try. Whilst making the job exciting the copy keeps its feet on the ground by a description in career terms of its worthwhileness and responsibility.

For further information, advertisements include an exhortation to visit a local RAF Careers Information Office, or to send in a coupon.

In its present form the campaign has run since June 1978.

EVALUATION OF THE CAMPAIGN

The enquiries generated each month by the range of aircrew advertisements between January 1978 and March 1980 have been analysed against the advertising expenditure for these months. The analysis shows that there is a correlation between advertising weight and the number of enquiries. The relationship is illustrated in Figure 16.1.

The *top* diagram in this chart shows monthly expenditure (both display and classified) in thousands of pounds at current prices, from January 1978 to March 1980 inclusive. The *bottom* diagram shows the numbers of enquiries received each month in hundreds.

For various reasons, one would not expect the two patterns to match exactly. For example the enquiries shown for each month include walk-ins to Careers Information Offices as well as return of coupons clipped from advertisements; and the monthly expenditure totals include different mixtures of display advertisements (full pages or double-page spreads) and

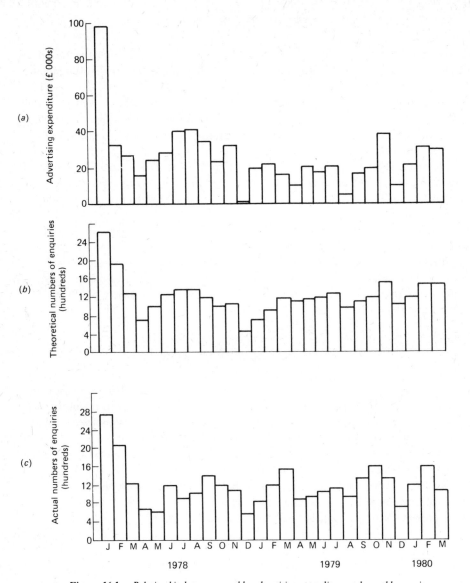

Figure 16.1. *Relationship between monthly advertising expenditure and monthly enquires.*

classified, which exhibit different levels of response per £ spent. Again, coupons from display advertisements tend to be returned a slightly longer time after their publication than those from classified advertisements. Furthermore, the ability to announce considerably improved rates of pay from March 1979 onwards raised the general levels of response after that time.

The *middle* diagram in Figure 16.1 shows the theoretical monthly pattern of returns, given the monthly pattern of advertising expenditure, once these other factors have been taken into account, and is helpful in predicting the level of enquiries which a given expenditure will generate. (The basis of this diagram is given in the appendix at the end of this chapter.)

Getting here
starts with a little application.

The first time in the Hawk we shot off down the runway, and went up like a lift. They said, "You won't know what's happening till you pass 10,000 feet."

Things were moving a lot more quickly than I was used to in the Provost. But after six hours, I was ready to go solo.

Of course you doubt yourself from time to time, but then you think of all the guys who've done it and before long you're up there with them. — *Graham Wardell*

FLT LT GRAHAM WARDELL, HAWK PILOT

COULD YOU BE A FLYER? Send this coupon to us now. We'll send you further information about Royal Air Force officer careers and an application form for our selection centre at Biggin Hill. If you really want to fly you must fill in this form. You may be just the man we want, but it's only by applying to see us that you'll know for sure.

WHAT WE LOOK FOR. In addition to your flying aptitude we are looking for initiative, leadership and, above all, a determination to succeed. Our training is designed to help you make the most of these qualities.

WHAT TO EXPECT The RAF offers you a very different lifestyle in a friendly and close-knit community, with the very best in sporting and social facilities. There is also the exhilaration of mastering a fast jet aircraft. But being an aircrew officer demands more than this.

The RAF is a vital part of NATO's defensive deterrent – we need dedicated officers to ensure it remains so.

SHORT SERVICE OR PERMANENT COMMISSION. The gratuity-earning Short Service Commission, for twelve years with an option to leave after eight, is now open to both pilots and navigators. The pensionable 16-year commission, with opportunities for further service, remains unchanged.

UNIVERSITY CADETSHIPS. You can also be sponsored by the RAF while you study at University or Polytechnic, through our University Cadetship Scheme.

If you would like to find out more about RAF Aircrew officer careers, get in touch with your local RAF Careers Information Office – address in phone book – or send in the coupon to Group Captain T. R. Morgan RAF Officer Careers, (xxxx/x), London Road, Stanmore, Middx. HA7 4PZ.

Please send me information about: Aircrew officer careers ☐ University Cadetships ☐

Name _____ Date of birth _____

(Age limits 17-23½)

Address _____

xxxx/x

Please enclose a separate note listing your present or intended qualifications. You must have 5 or more acceptable GCE O-levels at Grade C or above (or equivalent) including English Language and Maths. If you can offer A-levels or a degree, so much the better. Formal application must be made in the UK.

RAF officer

RAF press advertisement.

Figure 16.2 provides a similar illustration of the link between the monthly pattern of enquiries and the monthly pattern of returned application forms ('applications'). Here again the *top* and *bottom* diagrams show the actual numbers of enquiries and applications respectively received each month. The *middle* diagram (see Technical Notes) illustrates the theoretical monthly pattern of applications taking into account the time-lag between the receipt of an application form by an enquirer and its actual completion and return. The

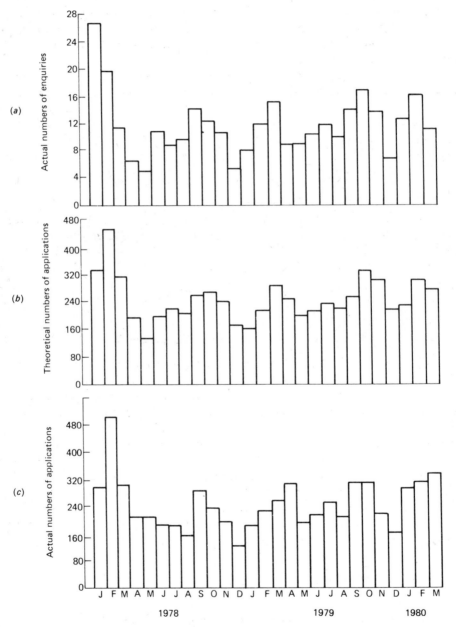

Figure 16.2.   *Relationship between monthly number of enquiries and monthly number of applications (in hundreds).*

correlation is high, which means that the enquiries generated are valuable ones which result in genuine applications.

But it is not simply quantity that is required, it is quality as well. The number of enquiries needed to achieve one pilot selection in 1978 was 41. In 1979 it was even lower, with only 35 enquiries needed. Both these levels are considered to be very good by the Royal Air Force in the light of their past experience.

The average media cost per enquiry in 1978 was £43, and since 41 enquiries were needed to achieve one selection the advertising cost of the selection can be calculated as 41 × £43, or only £1763. In 1979 the comparable cost figure was £1610. These are minute sums in relation to the high cost (c £1m) of training a pilot, and of the aircraft which stand idle if insufficient aircrew are recruited.

There is also evidence that advertising effectiveness is directly related to the communication of the right message, in an outstanding way. It is not just a case of being seen.

To illustrate the point about communicating the right message we can look at the different costs per enquiry 'scored' by different advertisements. Take the case of a full-page black and white advertisement which ran in 1976 without an illustration of an aircraft. Instead, it contained a satellite photograph of England, and the headline read:

'We want high flyers who want to fly higher'

The cost per enquiry for this advertisement was £233.

Learning from experience and research, in 1979 the campaign included two full-page black and white advertisements which incorporated two important changes – different illustrations and different headlines. Dramatic eye-catching photographs of aircraft were used – of a Tornado with the headline

'A 22 year old could fly it'

and of a Hawk with the headline

'Getting here starts with a little application'

The cost per enquiry for these advertisements was £79 and £95 respectively. If media inflation were taken into account, the true comparative costs would be even lower.

These differences represented substantial improvements to the message, making it a lot more relevant and involving to our target audience. The photograph of England from a great height was replaced by dramatic photography of military aircraft, which we knew appealed to potential candidates, and elitism was replaced by reassurance in the headline, to make the skills required more achievable.

To illustrate the point about communicating the message in an outstanding way, the 1979 advertisement 'Getting here starts with a little application' was first run as a single page in black and white. The cost per enquiry achieved was, as noted above, £95. It was then run as a double-page spread in colour – which highlighted more strongly the exciting and irresistible quality of flying. The cost per enquiry was reduced to only £59.

SUMMARY

In summary, we submit that the variable of advertising input has been demonstrated to bear a direct relationship with recruitment achievement.

The number of enquiries generated bears a remarkably direct relationship to advertising expenditure despite the existence of other variables; and the quality of response is seen to be related to the communication of the right message, in the right way.

APPENDIX: TECHNICAL NOTES

The middle diagram (*b*) in Figure 16.1 is based on the results of a statistical technique known as multiple regression. This technique examines how the changes in one particular series of observations – in this case, the number of enquiries received each month – are related to those of a number of other series – in this case, the monthly patterns of advertising expenditure in particular. In other words, the technique attempts to 'explain' the movements of one series in terms of the others.

The result of this analysis is a mathematical equation which describes this relationship in average terms on the basis of past experience. This equation contains one constant term and a series of other terms which allocate 'weights' to the variable factors (such as monthly advertising expenditure) which are being used to explain the original series.

The equation which we derived from such an analysis of the data for the 27-month period January 1978 to March 1980 was as follows:

Theoretical number of enquiries received 'this' month
=   365 (the constant term in the equation)
+   17.4 *times* display advertising expenditure 'this' month (in £'000s)
+   3.8 *times* display advertising expenditure 'last' month (in £'000s)
+   39.3 *times* classified advertising expenditure 'this' month (in £'000s)
+   390 for advertisements from March 1979 onwards incorporating the improved rates of pay.

It is these 'theoretical numbers of enquiries' which are plotted in diagram (*b*) of Figure 16.1.

The constant first term in the equation (365) presumably reflects the numbers of enquiries generated by sources of information on career opportunities in the RAF other than media advertising, as well as those contributed by sustained advertising over a long period. The next three terms reflect the average contribution made in the short term by the monthly expenditure on advertising. The final term (390) reflects the boost to the monthly numbers of enquiries apparently contributed by the offer of substantially increased rates of pay from March 1979 onwards.

Diagram (*b*) on Figure 16.2 is based on a similar type of analysis, this time relating the monthly numbers of *applications* to the numbers of enquiries received in previous months. The equation on which this diagram is based is as follows:

Theoretical number of applications received 'this' month
=   38 (the constant term in the equation)
+   .0976 *times* the number of enquiries 'this' month
+   .0813 *times* the number of enquiries 'last' month.

Section Four

Industrial and Financial

17

Lucas Aerospace 'Eagle' Campaign

INTRODUCTION

In this case study, we have tried to stress a number of important elements which contribute to an assessment of the campaign as both effective and successful:

In the Background section we first wanted to show that the campaign was *IMPORTANT* – not just to Lucas Aerospace but to Britain. Secondly, that the task Lucas Aerospace was facing was *ENORMOUS* – operating a £100m company in an incredibly competitive environment where most of the trends were against. Thirdly, that the advertising task was *DIFFICULT* – since the company was largely unknown in many market areas, competitors were spending much more on promotion and the product range to be covered was immense.

In the Objectives section we have been general (because of company security) about corporate objectives but specific about the advertising objectives including an understanding of the phased nature of the expected results of a campaign that has already been running $2\frac{1}{2}$ years. We also define target audiences and briefly cover budgets.

In the Campaign section we have described the media thinking which led us to the unusual conclusion to use only one publication incorporating a variety of spaces. Also described is the creative thinking which led to the 'eagle' concept and the subtle changing of headlines, copy, base lines and photographs as the campaign progressed.

In the Results section we have explained the commitments to results measurement from day one in December 1977; we have shown the way in which those results led to changes in the campaign in order better to achieve the objectives; we have actually listed results achieved, both numerate and non-quantifiable; and we have shown the progress of the company both to 1980 and beyond.

BACKGROUND

General

Since the mid-1950s, effectively until the coming of the Thatcher Government in 1979, successive British Governments have actively encouraged the amalgamation of separate companies into larger units more able to withstand US and European competition.

In 1957 Duncan Sandys, then Minister of Defence, when talking about the aviation industry said that he could envisage a day when Britain had only four major aerospace companies: one airframe manufacturer, one for helicopters, one for aero-engines and one dominant in the complex area of airframe and engine systems and equipment.

Now, in 1980, we have:

Airframes	—British Aerospace Corporation
Helicopters	—Westland
Aero-engines	—Rolls-Royce
Airframe and engine systems	—Lucas Aerospace

Lucas Aerospace

Lucas Aerospace was formed in 1971 from the combination of: Special Products Group of English Electric (formerly Aircraft Equipment Division), Rotax, Hobson, Lucas Gas Turbine Equipment Ltd., and, in 1974, the aircraft gas turbine business of Alvis. These constituent parts had existed mainly to service the UK aircraft industry, which had flourished in the immediate postwar years but in the 60s and 70s was suffering badly at the hands of, primarily, US competition.

The first major tasks of the new company were inward-looking: new structures of organization; rationalization of product ranges and manufacturing location; reassessment of research programmes and decisions as to where they should be carried out; and building a new morale and sense of corporate direction.

In addition, of course, the company had major marketing tasks.

Markets and Competition

Although a thoroughly international business, 80 per cent of the Western world's aerospace market is in North America. Consequently, Lucas desperately needed to become known and effective there (particularly the USA).

By the mid-70s Lucas Aerospace had reduced UK competition (i.e. from some separate companies in some fields of operation). It had, however, very significant competition worldwide, much of it based in North America.

MARKETS

The companies listed in Table 17.1 effectively make up the market for Lucas products.

The aerospace industry is, however, so made up that many additional points of influence

TABLE 17.1: MARKETS FOR LUCAS PRODUCTS

UK	Rest of Europe	N America
British Aerospace	Airbus Industrie	Boeing
Westland	Aerospatiale	Lockheed
Rolls-Royce	Panavia	McDonnell Douglas
		General Dynamics
		De Havilland of Canada
		Pratt & Whitney
		Avco Lycoming
		Sikorsky
		Hughes
		Bell
		Martin Marietta

Lucas Aerospace press advertisement. (This is the final page of the six-page advertisement.)

are brought to bear on marketing decisions from, for example, sub-contracting companies, airline operators, civil aviation authorities, etc.

COMPETITION

All four of those named as North American competitors in Table 17.2 are bigger than the whole of Lucas Industries Group, let alone Lucas Aerospace. What is more, they have a much larger proportion of their total business in the Aerospace field.

Lucas Aerospace plainly had an enormous task to establish itself as a genuine world-wide competitor in the aerospace industry.

TABLE 17.2: COMPETITORS OF LUCAS

UK	Rest of Europe	N America
Triplex (electrically heated windscreens)	Siemens	Westinghouse
Dowty (fuel controls)	Seconda Mona	Bendix
Hawker Siddeley Dynamics (fuel controls)	Nicro Turbo	Lear Siegler
		Sperry
		(and many others)

The Product Range

For largely historical reasons (i.e. the formation of Lucas Aerospace from the amalgamation of several other companies), Lucas had, and still has, the largest product range available from any airframe and engine systems supplier. Thus Lucas was smaller than many of its major competitors but did have a larger, more complete, product range. This made for some difficulties in production scale and R & D spread, but did have customer advantages. As far as promotion was concerned, it gave an obvious and important plus point, but there were complications as to possible dissipation of message.

The Selling Process

The selling process for Lucas Aerospace products in this particular industry is technically orientated, complex and covers a long time span. Each sale includes considerable discussions and negotiations concerning specifications, manufacturing methods, quality control, service and parts back-up and, of course, pricing and financing.

In addition, there are other influences upon the sale:

(a) Political – due to defence connotations and due to local purchase and local employment effects.
(b) Military – in the case of military projects, air force personnel will have an influence upon the airframe or engine builder.
(c) Commercial – in the case of non-military projects, airline personnel may also bring influence to bear upon the manufacturers.

Despite this, the number of potential customers and sources of influence remain small and it is the sort of market situation where many managements would have concluded that advertising could play no significant role for them.

Lucas Sales and Marketing Activity

World-wide marketing is led from head office in Birmingham under the control of the Sales and Marketing Director. There are UK and export sales and technical sales support personnel operating from Birmingham and there are subsidiary companies in Australia, USA and Canada.

In addition, and of considerable importance, are product support activities covering (a) *Commercial*: repair, overall overhaul, spares provisioning and emergency service, warranty administration; (b) *Engineering*: service engineering, technical publications, training, technical liaison. Product support centres exist in UK, Australia, Brazil, Canada, France, India, Japan, USA and West Germany.

OBJECTIVES

Lucas Aerospace corporate objectives have, of course, been developed and refined over the years since formation in 1971. A significant new direction can, however, be seen clearly since 1976–77. The company is unwilling to have details of corporate objectives made public. Stated broadly they are:

(a) Maintain market position in UK despite decline in the UK market.
(b) Develop market position in the rest of Europe.
(c) Build new market position in North America, where the world market largely resides.

For a year of so this did not reflect itself in revised and specific advertising objectives and plans.

In mid-1977 Nicklin Advertising developed for Lucas Aerospace a number of broad advertising objectives:

1. Develop higher familiarity with Lucas Aerospace name/company.
2. Develop higher favourable overall impression of company.
3. Develop higher favourable association with specific products/traits.

These objectives were part of the overall company objective: *Develop higher sales and a higher level of future contracts.*

The advertising audience was defined as:

(a) Corporate officers – airframe, engine and helicopter manufacturers, purchasing, engineering, finance, general management
(b) Engineers – manufacturers
(c) Senior managers and engineers – aircraft operators
(d) Senior and engineering officers – military (air forces)
(e) Academics – aerospace fields
(f) Politicians – aerospace interests

The budgets were to be very small both in absolute and comparative terms. Although we should not reveal exact details of promotional budgets, the following is the media spend during the period under consideration.

1978—£34 000
1979—£50 000
1980—Figures not yet available for the full year but in line with 1979

There were, in addition, occasional ad hoc advertisements covering events or special products.

THE CAMPAIGN

Media

PUBLICATIONS

Aviation Week and Space Technology was chosen as the sole publication to carry the campaign.

It stands head and shoulders above all other aerospace magazines whether British, French, Italian or American and is truly international in stature. Even coverage of the armed forces and defence markets is exceptionally good.

Aviation Week was, therefore, bound to be included in the media list, but it was chosen as the sole vehicle in order that Lucas Aerospace could appear as dominant as the limited budget would allow.

ADVERTISEMENT SIZE

At all times through the campaign, spaces have been varied to maximize on certain important effects:

(a) Appearance of size and dominance – hence multi-page advertisements in each of the Marketing Digest editions.
(b) Detailed presentation of technical products.

ADVERTISEMENT LOCATION

Nicklin discussed, for each advertisement, its location within the magazine and selected the best possible spaces, e.g. within a feature of particular relevance to Lucas Aerospace markets.

SPREAD

The Marketing Digest issue, published at the end of December each year, is much more than simply one issue of 50. It is a large volume detailing most suppliers to the aerospace industry and thereafter acts as a 'bible' to the industry for the following year.

Certain other issues have particular importance to Lucas Aerospace, for example, the issues that cover the Farnborough and Paris Air Shows.

Additionally, issues were selected which included Harvey Readership research so that judgements could be made as to the effectiveness of the advertising.

Other than these specials, the campaign has attempted to balance dominance and frequency with budget.

Creative

CONSIDERATIONS

(a) Product pictures should be 'real', i.e. photographic and colour. Product copy should be unashamedly technical and relating to the products in use. The assessment of the audience and the technical stature of the media led to the view that this creative approach would be more credible.

(b) Naturally the recently developed Lucas Industries Group 'green arrow' logostyle would be used in the advertisements.

(c) The other main creative element was to be the eagle, chosen because it was both dramatic and relevant.

Dramatic: overall bleed pictures, where appropriate, for dominance. Simply a dramatic subject. Real (rather than zoo) shots – graininess – drama.

Relevant: power in flight
beauty in flight
efficiency in flight
emotional, patriotic appeal to Americans (no negatives outside USA).

PROGRAMMES AND VARIATIONS

The campaign so far can be conveniently seen in three phases:

Phase 1. 1978 starting with the Marketing Directory edition of 19 December 1977.
Phase 2. 1979 starting with the Marketing Directory edition of 18 December 1978.
Phase 3. 1980 (to June) starting with the Marketing Directory edition of 31 December 1979

Phase 1. Maximum power, maximum effect with the first 'ad' of the campaign covering six pages. Thereafter fairly widely spaced double-half-page 'ads' covering various product ranges, approximately each alternate month on average, with a secondary boost of a larger space size in September to support Farnborough Air Show.

Phase 2. The campaign developed subtly in two ways. The Marketing Directory 'ad' was reduced slightly; thereafter a mixture of double-page and two consecutive right-hand-page 'ads', increasing in frequency to one per month. Also the message was slightly changed to associate Lucas Aerospace and the manufacturers as partnerships combining to do important things in aerospace.

Phase 3. Another subtle but important development, again in two areas, and adopting a more 'assumptive' stance, since, by now, the company's awareness and reputation had become better established in the market. Main emphasis now on monthly single-page 'ads' (plus major push in the Marketing Directory). The message is changed to a 'World leader' format associating Lucas Aerospace with specific product areas, with specific man-ufacturers and with specific military contracts and important international operators.

STRATEGIC AND TACTICAL

The campaign has primarily strategic objectives; the advertising was playing its part in an overall corporate plan. In addition, however, during phase 3 of the advertising it was used tactically to support and apply pressure on a major contract which was due for decision in April or May 1980. The relevant product advertisement was inserted in February and March issues, and the contract was awarded to the company shortly afterwards.

RESULTS

From the beginning, this campaign has been seen as one which would be judged by results and which would be altered according to results. It was also recognized that it would be difficult and expensive to be slavish about the assessment of the separate effect of various parts of the programme. None the less measurements have been applied wherever possible (economically sensible) and these have been used as *part of* the judgement process.

The Advertising Campaign

The response to every insertion has been recorded (although it was not primarily a response-orientated campaign) (Table 17.3). The greater part of this response has come through the chosen medium, *Aviation Week*, but is augmented by response direct to the company in the UK, in the US and elsewhere.

Study of these responses, together with knowledge that some product areas would be expected to 'pull' more than others, helped the decisions to switch from double half pages through double whole pages to single pages through the campaign.

Measurement of the responses has shown a very effective job done by the advertising programme in moving through the advertising objectives to 'favourable association with specific products'.

Phase 1	867 responses	£34K media spend	£39.2 per response
Phase 2	1511 responses	£50K media spend	£33.0 per response
Phase 3	960 responses in 6 months	not yet available	certain to be more cost effective than Phase 2

This is *without* any allowance for inflation and takes no account of the increasing sterling value of the market.

The geographical spread of the results has also been very satisfactory when associated with the markets that needed particular attack.

TABLE 17.3: RESPONSES TO ADVERTISING CAMPAIGN

	Insertion date	Responses
Phase 1	19 December 1977	453[a]
	13 March 1978	83
	17 April	61
	5 June	58
	3 July	52
	4 September	100
	20 November	60
Phase 2	18 December 1978	340[a]
	19 February 1979	94
	12 March	77
	30 April	217
	21 May	164
	11 June	65
	20 August	101
	24 September	96
	1 October	80
	22 October	87
	11 November	81
	26 November	62
	17 December	47
Phase 3	31 December 1979	304[a]
	21 January 1980 ⎫ 28 January ⎭	145
	3 March	60
	7 April	75
	21 April	200
	12 May	107
	19 May	69

[a] Marketing Directory.

Of the responses:

UK	7.9%
Europe	14.8%
N America	64.4%
Others	12.9%

As important as response statistics in assessing the effectiveness of the advertising are the non-quantifiable reactions of the company's staff, particularly sales, technical sales and product support people. These have, without exception, supported the campaign. They felt it materially altered prospects and customers' perceptions of Lucas over the period of the campaign. From being virtually unknown on any 'cold call' outside the UK, they are now seen everywhere as being one of the leading companies in the field in the whole world.

'OUR RECEPTION AND OUR CREDIBILITY ARE DRAMATICALLY ALTERED' (Lucas statement)

Regularly throughout the campaign (at approximately six-monthly intervals) Harvey Communication Measurement studies were done on advertisements appearing. (The

Marketing Directory multi-page 'ads' were not tested since they were so unusual they were felt unlikely to yield usable information.)

This research uses a standard recall technique carried out amongst *Aviation Week* readers by personal interview. It gives a measure of how one 'ad' compares with others in the issue in claimed recall and readership and it also gives a great deal of verbatim readers' comments which help in the assessment process:

Prior to the Campaign: Non-eagle 'ads' consistently scored lower than the 'issue average'. In February 1977, in response to the question 'How would you rate each of these companies as to the quality of their products and technical capability', 76 out of 100 people questioned answered 'Don't know' about Lucas Aerospace. Typical reader comments were:

'The message that I got had to do with how they provided support for the Concorde program. It tells about this part of the team that built the Concorde. This is a French company (sic) and we try to buy from US companies. If anyone were interested in working with a French company that is highly diversified in what they are doing, he might be interested in this.'
Director of Business Administration
Rocket Engines

'It does a very effective job in telling about the coordination of the countries in building and marketing this airplane. The desired result is to be able to fly to any country they want to. The ad is not very detailed or explicit, but it gets the point across.'
Strength Engineer
Fighter Equipment Manufacturer

'I have no need of their services at this time. I will keep them in mind for future consideration, though.'
Project Engineer
Aerospace Vehicles

By 1979 and 1980 Lucas Aerospace 'ads' were in every case scoring far higher recognition than the issue average, sometimes dramatically higher.

Typical readers were now much more knowledgeable about Lucas as well as more complimentary about the advertisements:

'This is a very impressive ad. The photograph is spectacular. The bird is so real and powerful-looking that it seems like it could step off the page. The large picture led me on, and then the smaller photo of the bird in flight united the two pages very well. It's a very good plan for a two page ad. Lucas is involved in engine management systems, and they are soliciting more business. They have a good record; all the big companies use them.'
Procurement Director
Aircraft

'Lucas is an old, established aircraft company. They basically deal in components, and they deal with all the major airlines in the world. I looked at the ad to see what was new. They're making components for first-class airplanes. That's what they do the best. Lucas is a very reliable stalwart, deeply-entrenched aircraft component company.'
Senior Process Engineer
Aircraft Forgings

'This advertisement gives a good input concerning their new product. I've seen their advertisements, but I've had no personal contact with the company.'
Vice President
Instrumentation R & D

'I've become familiar with the company's name through their previous advertisements. They project a strong image!'
President
Military Hardware R & D

'I didn't know that Lucas made an APU system. They seem capable. The picture caught my eye. From reading the ad, I get a good impression of the company. They've been in business for a long time, so I'd say they know what they're doing.'
Test Engineer
Flight Simulators

'As the advertisement mentioned, Lucas Aerospace manufactures jet fuel starters; I have heard the name 'Lucas' because they make our APUs, which are auxiliary power units. I also wanted to see what they had to do with the aircraft in the picture. I read the ad because I was seeking knowledge. If we use them, they must be good.'
Manager of Flight Services
International Airline

'The US Marine Corps depends on Lucas Aerospace's jet fuel starter and auxiliary power unit. They make highly reliable units.'
Engineer
Aircraft Components

'They've come up with an auxiliary power unit that responds well in an emergency. For example, if an engine stalls, this product can restart it again. Other companies make auxiliary power units, but Lucas has made theirs smaller and easier to control. I always look at their ads because an American eagle is always shown. This ad includes a small picture of the item. I am interested in finding out more about it.'
Production Manager
Custom Tooling

Least meaningful in measurement terms but one of the most gratifying responses of all has been the almost 100 people who have telephoned, written to, or spoken to Lucas Aerospace (over and above the product responses), asking for a picture of the eagle for their desk or wall. These have ranged from a US Senator to the wife of the President of one of the world's largest airframe manufacturers.

The Corporate Campaign

It is in this area that the results of the campaign really begin to mean something and they make a very powerful case.

Note 1. The corporate campaign can be said to date from the end of 1976. The advertising campaign started at the end of 1977. Time scales in this industry are extremely long.

Note 2. Although much detailed sales information is available, by time period, by geographical area and by product, all of which support the success of the campaign, the company is unwilling to have many of these figures made public. This is particularly true since, as a division of a large group, Lucas Aerospace information would not readily be available to competitors in any other form.

LUCAS AEROSPACE SALES (OFFICIAL FIGURES FROM LUCAS)

	Index
1976 — £88.8m	100
1977 — £89.4m	104
1978 — £101m	118
1979 — £117.4m	137
1980 — £157m (estimate)	177

These sales figures include some important areas of past sales in dramatic decline because of the decline in aircraft or engine production.

LUCAS AEROSPACE NORTH AMERICAN SALES

Prior to 1976 there was a negligible level of direct sales: mainly parts to back-up products sold to engine makers (Rolls-Royce) and then shipped to the USA. Now Lucas Aerospace sales to North America are well over 10 per cent of the total sales (i.e. more than £15m in 1980) and it is expanding very fast.

LUCAS AEROSPACE CONTRACTS

Since 1977 and growing progressively, Lucas has won the following contracts, many of which will go on for 10 to 20 years:

McDonnell Douglas	—	Harpoon missile capsule
McDonnell Douglas	—	Harpoon missile actuator
De Havilland of Canada	—	Dash 7 (aircraft)
Canadair	—	Challenger (aircraft)
Sikorsky	—	S-76 Spirit helicopter
Boeing Vertol	—	CH 47D Chinook helicopter
Lockheed	—	Tristar
Boeing	—	746 and 767

All these are direct contracts (i.e. not those via Rolls-Royce).

In addition, it was announced in April 1980 that Lucas Aerospace had won a giant contract from Avco Lycoming for fuel control systems for helicopter engines. The contract is expected to lead to orders totalling at least £18m, and possibly double that, over the next ten years.

18

Halifax Building Society Convertible Term Shares

BUSINESS BACKGROUND

The Funding of Mortgages

The function of building societies today is basically no different from when they were established in the mid-nineteenth century. They simply exist to lend money to people who wish to buy their own homes. That money is lent at a certain rate of interest which is higher than the interest rates paid to the building society investors, whose savings fund the mortgages. The difference between the two rates pays the building societies' costs and overheads and government tax. The very small amount of surplus remaining is used to maintain liquid reserves.

It has not been necessary, since prewar days, for building societies to market mortgages. The desire for home ownership in the UK has risen dramatically since the war. In 1945 26 per cent of homes were owner occupied. By 1978 that figure had increased to 53.9 per cent.

As the demand for mortgages grew it became necessary for the societies to attract more funds in the form of personal savings to enable them to meet this demand. They have achieved a not unreasonable success. In 1950 the number of share (savings) accounts with all building societies totalled 2 256 000: by 1978 the number of accounts had increased to 24 999 000. Early in 1980 about 55 per cent of the population aged over 16 possessed one or more building society share accounts.

There is no doubt that the considerable sums spent by all building societies on promotional activity during the last 10 years have played a large part in educating the public into the desirability of saving through building societies. However, the very success of all this activity has brought its own problems. In 1960 less than two savers were needed to finance one borrower: currently five savers are needed.

There are two main reasons for this escalation. One is that the supply/demand situation for home ownership has led to the cost of private housing overtaking that of inflation: therefore, in relative terms, borrowers require larger mortgages. Secondly, and perhaps more important, the building societies' successful penetration into the savings market has meant that more and more smaller savers have been drawn into the net. These two factors have combined to create the five savers = one mortgage situation mentioned above.

The funding of mortgages during any one year is accomplished mainly from three sources: (a) net inflow in shares and deposits (savings), (b) mortgage capital repayments, and (c) mortgage interest payments. The net inflow is that amount which is left after depositors have withdrawn some of the funds which were originally on deposit. 'Gross receipts' (the measure of all money which is deposited with a building society during any one year) far exceeds net inflow. For instance, during 1979 gross receipts into all building societies totalled £18 940 million. Of that amount £15 614 million was withdrawn again, leaving only £3326 million as 'net inflow' for the funding of mortgages.

Term Shares vs. Ordinary Shares

The bulk of any building society's gross receipts is made up from two types of shares or savings plans: term shares (approximately 13 per cent) and ordinary shares (approximately 80 per cent). Ordinary shares currently pay the investor 10.5 per cent net interest, but he/she is able to withdraw money virtually at will and it is this type of share account that suffers badly when building society interest rates become uncompetitive with the clearing banks or when, for instance, a new issue of National Savings Bonds carrying a higher interest rate is announced.

Term shares, on the other hand, are far more stable. Once money is deposited it cannot normally be withdrawn before the agreed term has expired. This is compensated for in terms of higher interest rates – up to 2 per cent above the ordinary rate in the case of five-year term shares.

Building Society Costs and Administration

Since a building society's ability to lend money for mortgages is dependent upon that amount remaining – the net inflow (the difference between receipts and withdrawals) – it would seem that the more stable term share money it can attract the better. However, although building societies do not make a profit in the normally accepted commercial sense, long term share money is, in effect, a loss maker because of the higher interest rates payable. Let's take a very simplified look at the average costs of financing a straightforward mortgage at the rate of 15 per cent p.a. through an ordinary share account and a term share account (Table 18.1).

TABLE 18.1: BUILDING SOCIETY COSTS

	Ordinary share	Five-year term share
Charge to borrower	15%	15%
Paid to Investor	10.5%	12.5%
Tax	2.0%	2.0%
B.S. operating cost	0.9%	0.9%
Surplus	1.6%	−0.4%

As has been said, the above table is simplified and does not take into account, for instance, the lower cost of servicing term share accounts. However, it serves to illustrate the fact that the one type of share can subsidize the other. The trick is to maximize total inflow from both types of account consistent with producing enough surplus to maintain the ratio of reserves or liquid funds to the increasing value of assets.

An easy way to Xtra high interest.

Halifax Convertible Term Shares are specially designed for the investor with a lump sum of £500 or more who wants top rates of interest but may not wish to tie up his money for a long period. In many ways it's like going up in a lift.

You can choose to get out where you like.

To come into the scheme you need only commit your money for as short a period as one year.

Or you can choose any longer period of years from 2 to 5. In which case we'll pay you even better rates of interest.

You can go straight to the top rate.

By choosing an initial term of 5 years you'll receive our best rate of interest from the very beginning.

You could stay in for longer.

After the initial term you have the option of taking your money out or leaving it with us, subject to three months' notice of withdrawal, at premium rates which will go up year by year until the top rate is reached.

By the fifth year your money will be earning 2% above the Paid-up Share rate. And it goes on earning that top premium for as long as it stays in the scheme.

That's the beauty of Halifax Convertible Term Shares. They're so flexible.

You can plan your saving to suit your own specific requirements while still getting an excellent return on your investment.

But then, isn't that the kind of scheme you'd expect from the biggest building society in the world?

Current Interest Rates.

Term of Years	1	2	3	4	5
Rate of Interest Payable*	11.00%	11.25%	11.50%	12.00%	12.50%
Gross Equivalent Rate**	15.71%	16.07%	16.43%	17.14%	17.86%

Withdrawal after the initial term is completed is subject to three months' notice either by you or by the society.
Maximum total holding in the society is £20,000 for an individual, £40,000 for a joint account.

SEND IN THIS COUPON NOW FOR OUR HIGHEST INTEREST RATE EVER. To: Halifax Building Society, (Ref. I.K.W.), P.O. Box 60, Trinity Road, Halifax HX1 2RG

I/We enclose a cheque, numbered _____ for £ _____
MIN.INVESTMENT £500
To be invested in: TICK APPROPRIATE BOXES

☐ 5 YEAR ☐ 4 YEAR ☐ 3 YEAR ☐ 2 YEAR ☐ 1 YEAR CONVERTIBLE TERM SHARES
The interest to be:
☐ added to balance subject to the maximum total holding ☐ paid half-yearly ☐ paid monthly (min. investment £1,000)

I/We understand that the investment cannot be withdrawn before the initial term has expired except in the case of death.

FULL NAME(S)

ADDRESS

SIGNATURE(S)

_____ DATE

Get a little Xtra help with the future.

HALIFAX BUILDING SOCIETY, P.O. Box 60, TRINITY RD, HALIFAX HX1 2RG

*CONVERTIBLE TERM SHARES INCLUDE A GUARANTEED PREMIUM (IN ADDITION TO THE CURRENT PAID-UP SHARE RATE WHICH IS VARIABLE) OF 2% FOR 5 YEAR, 1.50% FOR 4 YEAR, 1.00% FOR 3 YEAR, 0.75% FOR 2 YEAR AND 0.50% FOR 1 YEAR SHARES. AFTER THE INITIAL TERM THE GUARANTEED PREMIUM INCREASES ANNUALLY UNTIL THE MAXIMUM OF 2% IS REACHED IN THE FIFTH AND SUBSEQUENT YEARS. **THE ABOVE GROSS RATES OF INTEREST APPLY IF YOU PAY INCOME TAX AT THE BASIC RATE OF 30%.

Halifax Building Society Convertible Term Shares press advertisement.

MARKETING OBJECTIVE

In the Spring of 1979 the Halifax Building Society decided that the term share department could afford to accept an increase in funds over and above the £130 million which, on a historical basis, had been previously estimated as the amount of *new* account term share receipts which would be taken during the year ending 31st January 1980. It was felt that an increase of 50 per cent would be a not unreasonable objective and that this would still be consistent with the Society producing a healthy surplus. Thus an objective of £195 million gross receipts into *new* term shares was set.

New Product

The marketing department recommended that the above objective could be met only if a new Halifax product which gave investors the opportunity to achieve a maximum interest rate without having to 'sign up' for the maximum period could be developed and launched. They further recommended that the launch should be backed by a heavy advertising campaign.

And so '*Convertible Term Shares*' were designed.

A 'Convertible Term Share' is, in effect, a 'roll-over' share, specially designed for the investor with a lump sum of £500 or more who wants top rates of interest but may not wish to tie his money up for a long period. To join the scheme an investor need only commit his money for as short a period as one year. This currently pays him net interest of 10.75 per cent. After the initial period has expired he can take his money out or leave it with the Society, subject to three months' notice of withdrawal, at premium rates which will go up year by year until the top rate of 12.50 per cent is reached. An investor can, of course, choose any longer period of years from two to five at the start, in which case he receives the higher rate of interest from day one. When he reaches the end of year five he has the option of leaving his money with the Society for as long as he wishes, still earning the top rate of interest of 12.50 per cent. The interest earned can either be added to the balance, paid half-yearly or paid monthly.

Note: Had an investor opted for the five-year period from day one he would, in effect, have bought a 'five-year term share' – a product which already existed but had not yet been promoted by the Society.

Advertising Objectives

The first objective had to be to create as high an awareness as possible, as quickly as possible, for the new product. It was agreed that a heavyweight campaign on TV would be the best way to achieve this.

However, this was a somewhat complicated proposition and 'selling', as distinct from awareness, would need to be done off the page. At this stage the agency put forward another recommendation. In view of the client's lack of experience of product sell, the agency suggested that all press advertisements should be couponed. And not only couponed, but should ask for money. We had no idea at this stage, of course, whether people would cut out a coupon, pin to it a cheque for £10 000 and send it off to the other end of the country! However, if it worked, it could give us a great deal of useful information regarding media effectiveness and, on an ongoing basis, would allow us to test creative platforms at the sharp end. No one expected that all inflow would be achieved off the page of course; all we were hoping for was a large enough percentage to enable us to make viable judgements for the future.

Media Strategy

As already indicated, TV was chosen as a method to create high awareness quickly. In terms of the market for whom the product would have maximum appeal – i.e. the financially aware ABC1s – the press schedule included the quality dailies and Sundays, but not, at this stage, the popular press. In phase one of the campaign, due to break on 1st August and to last six weeks, a budget of £270 000 was agreed, £150 000 for TV and £120 000 for press.

The Unforeseen Delay

We were now into late June and plans were well advanced. Then the agency was advised that the BSA, to whom building societies need to give notice of all new products, would not be in a position to give approval to convertible term shares until mid-August.

The Halifax Building Society's marketing department, in view of the now urgent requirement for more term share inflow, decided to substitute, temporarily, a five-year term share (a product which had already been approved by the BSA) campaign to run in place of the convertible term share campaign.

Television Strike

This campaign ran as planned – successfully. However, before we were able to start the original TV campaign for convertible term shares the TV strike came along. So convertible term share advertising ran without benefit of TV in press only until 1st January 1980. The various bursts of promotional activity and their costings were eventually as follows:

Period	Product	Budget
August 1st–15th 1979	'Five-year' term shares	£104 000 TV
		£80 000 press
August 16th–mid-Sept. 1979	'Convertible' term shares	£300 000 press
January 1st–31st 1980	'Convertible' term shares	£250 000 TV
		£150 000 press

CAMPAIGN EVALUATION

We believed that we could make a fair assessment of the value of the campaign only if we excluded all factors that might not have been affected by advertising. Therefore, whenever we refer to term share gross receipts in this section, we mean only gross receipts which are attributable to new account openings. We have excluded that percentage of receipts which comes from the re-investment of existing maturing term shares, transfers of money from other types of account and also the interest credited.

Firstly then, we made a comparison between the growth of new term share gross receipts and the growth of all gross receipts during the years 1977, 1978 and 1979 (Table 18.2).

This table shows that the growth of term share gross receipts had consistently not shown anything like the growth rate of total gross receipts. Even the introduction of a new three-year term share in May 1977 (unsupported by advertising) had virtually no effect (Table 18.3).

TABLE 18.2: NEW TERM SHARE GROSS RECEIPTS AGAINST ALL GROSS RECEIPTS

	Jan. 31st 1977 £m	Jan. 31st 1978 £m	Jan. 31st 1979 £m
Gross receipts (all depts.)	2063.6	2628.9	3011.2
% Increase		+27%	+15%
Gross receipts (term shares)	100.2	106.1	113.8
% Increase		+6%	+7%

TABLE 18.3: NEW TERM SHARE GROSS RECEIPTS

	1976 £m	1977 £m	% Change	All receipts % change
1st Quarter	28.7	22.8	−21	+1
2nd Quarter	25.5	26.3 (new three-year term share)	+3	+27
3rd Quarter	26.6	28.5	+7	+7
4th Quarter	20.6	24.9	+21	+43

Related to historical growth and the Society's projected estimated growth of total gross receipts by 20 per cent for year end 31st January 1980, it was estimated that, without advertising support, gross receipts into new term shares for the same year would grow by 16 per cent to £130m (see Table 18.4). This was deliberately optimistic as the Society felt it was likely that the introduction of a new longer period term share carrying a relatively higher interest rate would result in more public interest.

TABLE 18.4: % GROWTH IN TERM SHARE GROSS RECEIPTS AS AGAINST ALL GROSS RECEIPTS

Year ending 31st January	All receipts	Term shares
1978	27	6
1979	15	7
1980	20 (estimated)	16 (estimated)

However, during the first two months of 1979 the growth of total gross receipts slowed down to 13 per cent, thus making the 16 per cent estimate for term shares seem even more optimistic. An indication of the strength of advertising in this context came in March 1979 when four-year term shares were introduced with a modest advertising budget of £25 000. New term share gross receipts for that month were some 84 per cent higher than in the same month a year previously. The impact was not sustained and growth rates tailed off in successive months.

So, in August 1979, the first product campaign for five-year term shares was launched, rapidly followed by the convertible term share campaign. By the year end an advertising investment of £884 000 had achieved the following:

	Original estimate	Target set	Achieved
New term share gross receipts	£130m	£195m +50%	£209m +61%

Therefore, new term share gross receipts had exceeded:

— the previous year by *83 per cent*
— the original estimate by *61 per cent*
— the target by *14 per cent*

or, in absolute terms:
— the previous year by *£96m*
— the original estimate by *£79m*
— the target by *£14m*

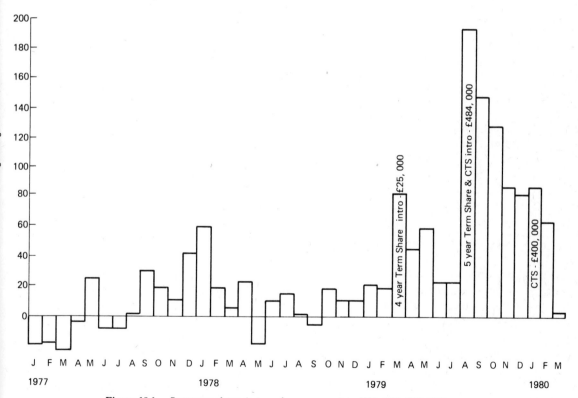

Figure 18.1. *Percentage change in term share gross receipts:* 1977, 1978, 1979, 1980.

However, if we need further proof of the effectiveness of the campaign, remember that the advertising activity took place during the six months 1st August 1979 to 31st January 1980. So let's compare that period with the previous six months.

		Original Estimate	Achieved	Increase
New term share gross receipts	1st Feb. 1979–31st July 1979	£65m	£78m	£13m
	1st Aug. 1979–31st Jan. 1980	£65m	£131m	£66m
		£130m	£209m	£79m

Therefore, £66m extra has been realized in the six months ending 31st January 1980.

Figure 18.1 shows the pattern of percentage change in term share receipt growth during the advertising bursts.

Cost Effectiveness

£884 000 yielded £66 million extra or £1 advertising yielded £75 investment

As far as the total Halifax balances are concerned (this does include transfers and credited interest), the effect was:

(a) to increase term share balances by 62 per cent,
(b) to increase the proportion of total balances accounted for by term shares from 8.5 to 11.7 per cent.

Thus the Halifax Building Society had achieved its broader objective of taking a larger share of inflow in term share money in an effort to overcome some of the problems of withdrawals of large amounts of short term (ordinary) funds. It is also worth mentioning that, in human terms, the extra £66m generated meant that the Halifax was able to grant 5300 more mortgages than it would otherwise have done.

Couponing of Press Advertisements

Finally, what did we learn from the couponing of our press advertisements? This turned out to be a very valuable part of the exercise. Firstly, we found that a surprisingly large number of people were prepared to open accounts by post and to send quite large amounts by cheque to the building society's head office. In some cases, even, the then maximum amount of £30 000 for a joint account was received by mail.

The agency's hope that the coupon response would allow us to make an evaluation of media effectiveness was also realized. Although, towards the end of the six-month campaign period, inflow from both branch offices and coupons was becoming depressed due to the uncompetitive building society interest rates then prevailing, relative media effectiveness remained, on the whole, fairly consistent.

Part way through the campaign a number of test insertions were booked in the popular press and, as expected, the coupon response in this area turned out to be very poor compared with the quality press. An index is attached (see Table 18.5) and the base of 100 relates to the average return across all media for each advertising £ spent.

The information gained has enabled us to weight our term share media schedule for 1980 in favour of the most cost-effective publications. Interestingly enough, again as we suspected, work done to date during the 1980 period has proved that couponed advertising for ordinary shares produces a much better response in the popular press than that we obtained for the term share product.

TABLE 18.5: RELATIVE EFFECTIVENESS OF MEDIA IN TERMS OF RETURN THROUGH COUPONS PER £1 OF ADVERTISING EXPENDITURE. INDEX OF 100 = AVERAGE RETURN OVERALL

Daily Telegraph	253
Sunday Telegraph	172
Guardian	167
Sunday Express	103
Daily Mail	94
Observer	90
Daily Express	69
Daily Star	63
Sunday People	37
Sun	29
Daily Mirror	23
Sunday Mirror	21
News of the World	12
Financial Times	9

Index

Numbers in *italics* refer to illustrations